The Jesus Story

Edmund Flood

Sheed & Ward

Sheed & Ward™ is a service of National Catholic Reporter Publishing
Company, Inc.

Library of Congress Catalog Card Number: 90-62088

ISBN: 1-55612-404-X

Published by: Sheed & Ward
                115 E. Armour Blvd. P.O. Box 419492
                Kansas City, MO 64141-6492

To order, call: (800) 333-7373

Contents

Introduction

Jesus of Nazareth

There is no reasonable doubt that Jesus lived in Palestine and died as an executed criminal.

Although most of our knowledge of him covers no more than three years, no personality in history has attracted so much interest. People of all faiths, as well as atheists, have felt the fascination of his values, his sayings, and the way he lived. But many of us don't find it easy to form a clear impression of Jesus' life and personality. His sayings sometimes seem at odds with one another or with his way of life. It can be difficult to see him as a fully human person. Some recent TV programs and films have only added to an understandable confusion.

This confusion, ironically, has recently become unnecessary, to a great extent. Of course, our understanding of any person is always incomplete, and still more when the person is of Jesus' stature and lived 2000 years ago. But biblical scholarship now allows us to understand Jesus much more fully than ever before.

This book seeks to make available to Christians and non-Christians the portrait of Jesus that scholarship yields. It should help us answer the kind of question we ask about any man or woman we find interesting or fascinating. We want to know what his or her aims were, and about how his or her contemporaries reacted to that person. How far did he or she succeed, and why? What about his or her failures? How did he or she understand and feel about their own lives and the people they cared about?

Through such questions we get at the thrust, the central thread, of any person's life. We discover what "makes them tick": their inner dynamism and achievement.

This portrait will be valuable, of course, only to the extent that it is true and honest. There won't be the space to discuss the opinions on the various areas of Jesus' life. Instead I shall present what the best recent scholarship seems to be roughly agreed upon. In some of the more contentious areas—like Jesus' miracles and resurrection—we'll step back from the portrait and take time to scrutinize the evidence on which it is based.

The result should be a fairly accurate picture of a person we can recognize to be as human as ourselves, and whose purpose, experience and relevance we can better discern.

One

First Months in Capharnaum

One day in 28 or 29, Jesus turned south off the imperial highway from Galilee to Damascus and entered the little fishing town of Capharnaum.

The buildings had the air of a 19th-century slum. They were all built from the coarse, drab basalt stones that lay scattered around. But with the hills behind, and the fields on either side going down to the lake, the setting was beautiful, especially in the spring.

It was obviously going to be a very different experience from those 30 years in Nazareth or his time in the desert. In this village you felt much more exposed to "the world." True, it didn't have the grandeur of Jerusalem or the modern sophistication of Tiberias. But people from different countries regularly passed along the highway or stopped for a while; and the town's inhabitants, though largely fisherfolk, included quite a wide range of other occupations as well. And Tiberias itself was only 10 miles away.

The feeling that he was in a very different world from Nazareth increased as Jesus walked down the main street. It ran from north to south down to the lakefront. Unlike the haphazard arrangement at Nazareth, the streets were laid out in an orderly grid. Criss-crossing the main street were a number of small alleys.

In one of these blocks was the house where Jesus stayed. On the left of the road, 30 meters from the synagogue, was the home of Peter, which Jesus could use.

That house would be very important to him in the months that lay ahead. To someone in the Western world today it might have seemed less like a home than a primitive barracks. You went through a doorway in the street into an L-shaped courtyard. Onto it opened three rooms, each a home for one family. The courtyard was the shared kitchen, with ovens set into it. In the long summer months, with temperatures often at 95°F, it was also a shared bedroom for the three houses: you simply spread a mat on the floor in the hot night air.

Much less "comfortable," of course, were the six or seven weeks of rain round the end of the year. Then you had to sleep in your family's one room, with the water from the nearby lake under the basalt stones beneath you, and the strong rains beating on the light roof above.

Few people in Capharnaum had any money to spare. Fish were abundant in that part of the lake, and the tackle to catch them was by now sophisticated. But with the state and the religious taxes, it was subsistence wages for most, and with a run of bad luck, poverty soon stared you in the face.

It was in this small town of about a thousand inhabitants that Jesus embarked on a course of action so different from his life up to now. He had no pat way of describing what it was. There would be a central slogan—easily and dangerously misunderstood; there would be his stories, his actions, and of course his personality. That was the "data" that he asked you to judge. There would be no beating of ideological drums: no strong-arm tactics forcing anyone's conscience. The only kind of response he was interested in was wholehearted and free. What kind of person did he seem to be in his first weeks in Capharnaum?

First Impressions

People quickly picked up a whole range of strong impressions. Jesus seemed to differ from others in a number of ways, some of them attractive, some controversial, some even repugnant.

He lived cut off from his family, and his main occupation was religion. In the Sabbath services in the synagogue—where any man could preach—people were struck by the freshness and power of his preaching. His journeys to preach in other towns and villages raised certain questions. They seemed to place him in the class of those wandering charismatic preachers who had felt a "call" to change the world. Already there was about Jesus a tinge of the revolutionary—an impression that would become much stronger as he became better known.

We show our set of values by the company we keep. With a Jew, that was especially declared by the people they were prepared to eat with. Having a meal with others, in the East, expressed loyalty and strong friendship. It has a seriousness that could be called "religious." To be disloyal to someone you have eaten with is seen as unspeakable.

Meals in those houses, of course, could not be private affairs. Before long many people had shared or looked in at the meals Jesus had. They were able to share their feelings about them with others. Their impressions formed a topic of fierce controversy in the little town.

A Meal with Jesus

What would happen if you accepted an invitation to one of his meals? Your first impressions might be very ordinary. The rough surface under your feet was of the large black basalt stones. The "rock-garden" effect reminded you of the poverty of the place.

The walls consisted of stones of the same kind stuck on top of each other. Because of the cheapness of the building, no mortar had been used, so that the walls could support only a roof of wooden beams and beaten earth mixed with straw. The rough simplicity of this way of life was evident in this and other ways.

Equally evident, all the same, was an air of festivity. In the courtyard you had already seen activity at the oven. Perhaps a batch of fish, caught that day, lay there ready to be cooked. Carafes of the strong local wine had been laid out in the room.

It was when you had been in the room for a while that the air of happiness became more comprehensible. It was incomplete, and somewhat hesitant, and there were strong pockets of resistance. But however insecure it still was, it arose from Jesus' relationship with these people.

The small room was crowded, which brought everyone there close. Some looked convinced: eager for what was to come. Others were plainly doubtful. But all seemed to be drawn, to some degree, by what they saw in Jesus: his warmth, his concern, and his infectious sense of peace.

All were aware that he was more than a comfortable, concerned friend. He seemed to be fired by the conviction that the world had now reached the time of great harvest and the moment of truth.

What it was that he longed for might not be clear for a time. But his sense of closeness to a great new dawn was a major part of what people saw.

The few windows were too high to let in much light, and evening was advancing. But as your eyes became used to the ill-lit room, you could gauge more clearly what your fellow guests seemed to feel.

On some faces there was obvious pleasure at spending a long, leisurely evening with Jesus and old friends. In others there was distrust, resentment, perhaps even some hatred. That was caused by the company they saw they were now to dine with.

The presence of toll-collectors[1] could be the main cause of grievance. Probably some people there had no great problem about their presence. Everyone knew how difficult it was to make a living. Whether you were in the town or in the country,

---

1. The people concerned seem to have been toll-collectors, not tax-collectors; and not to have been (as has commonly been thought) "collaborators" with the Roman government.

financial ruin was an ever-present threat. If ruin did come, you and your family became slaves. Your human dignity, and all you had, would have vanished—probably forever. Face-to-face with such a crisis, the job of a toll-collector could be your only chance of escape.

But others round the table saw the toll-collectors' presence very differently. They believed it was an affront, an intolerable outrage.

Everyone knew that toll-collecting was built on fraud. Someone with the necessary capital would buy from the Galilean government the right to collect the tolls in this area. He would have to pay a certain sum; but there was no guarantee that he would recoup it. If he was to avoid a loss, and indeed to make a profit, he might have to increase the tariff above the legal limit. And, of course, if he was unscrupulous, that likelihood increased.

The penalties for this kind of fraud could easily lead to bankruptcy, so it would probably be necessary to grease a few official palms. The result was that the local trader saw people who had grown fat in this "unnatural," corrupt way. Because the local official had been bribed, they had no choice but to pay the illegal tariffs. They and their families' chance of economic survival had become a helpless fly in the cruel web of the toll-system. Surely a toll-collector was an abomination to true religion? And Jesus had invited some of them to his meal tonight.

A word or two in the street with such people might have been tolerable. But here you were being invited to join with them in what Jesus was doing—to be fellow-members of Jesus' "family."

Yes, in a meal you bound yourself to a strong fellowship. But how could you be expected to do that with this scum?

Yes, you could feel the great attractiveness of Jesus, and perhaps, already, of his message. But did his inviting these toll-collectors show there was something unbalanced about the man?

And the same doubt could arise from the presence of women.

Jesus' Women Guests

The full scale of the problem of Jesus and women would not become clear until later in Jesus' story. But already, this evening, there were strong hints of what would come. At the supper table you saw that some women were present. You would have heard that Jesus' custom was to invite them to his parties. From a late 20th-century viewpoint, nothing of course could be more normal. But no one round that table could see it in that way.

To a Jew of Jesus' time, a woman was an inferior person who was expected to confine her activities to the family. The list of what women weren't allowed to do reads like rules for a bad prison.

They could be married without their consent. They could be divorced because they had cooked a bad meal, but could not demand a divorce from their husbands, whatever the situation. Some rabbis pronounced them incapable of being a valid witness in a court of law. A contemporary of Jesus' later expressed the common view: "a woman is in every respect of less worth than a man."[2]

In the sphere of religion, women's role had become extremely restricted. The restriction had originally arisen in a crisis situation where Israel was struggling to hold onto its belief that there is only one God. For Israel, the world is not a battleground of warring forces. Our lives are not at the mercy of blind or malicious "gods." We are governed, instead, by a wise and loving ruler: the only true God who had been found active in their story.

This forced Israel to reject the worship of the Nature goddess. The feminine in God became largely lost to view. As a result it was lost in the practices of religion. Women could not become priests or enter the main part of the Temple.

The suppression of the feminine became worse through another related factor. Israel wanted to appreciate the sheer holiness of God. God had a beauty and splendor beyond anything we can know. The naive way of suggesting "otherness" was to cut

---

2. Josephus

God off from the "merely" physical. So Jewish priests could not sacrifice if they had had sexual intercourse. On this view, women's periods made them ineligible for priesthood and other religious roles.

With all this went a profound distrust of people's morality. Since their sexual desires were considered uncontrollable, women must be confined to home as much as was possible. When they had to emerge from the home, they must be kept at a distance and their beauty hidden by their coiffures.

As the men round Jesus' table found women there too, they were bound to ask whether deeply-held viewpoints would not be flouted. Here was more than Jesus' easy familiarity with women that people saw in the Capharnaum streets. This wasn't just "conversation"; it was intimate and religious. Jesus was subverting their deeply-held values. By what right was he doing this, and where would it lead?

Part of the attraction of eating with Jesus was the way such questions were discussed. He didn't teach from a book or from a platform; he didn't bawl out demands. He was by your side at the table, for long, relaxed evenings. Over the food and the wine, there would be laughter and stories, questions, and discussion. You were there to be yourself, and speak from your own standpoint. With Jesus you were always more a guest than a pupil.

Since each individual there was important, the meal might start with introductions. Jesus wanted to know your past, your circumstances, and your deepest fears and hopes. He wanted to let you see these in the light of his own.

Two

The Heart
of the Message

After the introductions, the center of attention became Jesus.

Who was he? Why had he come to Capharnaum? Why did he hold these controversial meals? The men and women round Jesus' table had begun to form some answers. The fascination of the evening would be to sift them and take them further.

In the intimate, relaxed atmosphere, candid questions were no problem. Jesus was glad to share with them his own life story.

He was probably the only one round the table who had been to Nazareth, but many knew the style of life of small, remote towns. Near the top of its hill, away from the main routes, it seemed to them almost cut off from contemporary movements. They could visualize the terraced plots along the hillside, worked the same way, no doubt, for countless generations. Even in this bare Capharnaum house, they could feel "superior" to even the best homes of the Nazareth families.

Jesus described them as cave-like, cut out from the hillside. His home, like the rest, had been lit only from the door, and from the flicker of the oil lamps on the dark rugged walls. It was easy to imagine the atmosphere in the long, hot summer nights, as the family shared their house with its sheep, goats and hens.

Of course, even Nazareth could not be entirely immune from the events of the times. Hadn't the Sepphoris disaster happened only three miles away? Jesus had been only three when that city had been burnt to the ground, but many from his village would have witnessed the scene. They had only to climb the last 90 meters of the south side of the hill to see, down below to the north, Sepphoris being devoured by the flames. This was its punishment from a Roman general for conniving with a rebel against Herod's despotic rule. This memory of brutish Roman power would long remain vivid.

Jesus had quite early been introduced to the realities of his country's situation. Even as a boy he would have walked to the by-now rebuilt Sepphoris, flaunting its Romaness to show who was master. The city's size and sophistication were so different from Nazareth—its Roman theatre alone could have seated, 20 times over, all Nazareth's inhabitants.

In Jesus' adolescence and young adulthood, there had been other journeys in Galilee. Its ruler, Herod Antipas, was building a new capital at Tiberias only miles from Nazareth. As a carpenter and builder, Jesus would work there and in other cities along the west shore of the lake of Gennesaret.

As Jesus' guests pieced together the main facts of Jesus' background, his choice of Capharnaum began to make good sense.

Nazareth could not be chosen for a number of reasons. Someone with a message for his whole nation could not be heard in such a remote village; and with its deeply traditionalist outlook, it would not welcome new ways.

The Upper Galilee highlands to the north of it were even more remote. A city or town on a major road would be the right kind of base.

Sepphoris was too Roman, as well as too close to Nazareth. Tiberias was the most Roman of them all; and Jesus' talk of a "Kingdom" would have led to rapid extinction in Herod's capital.

But Capharnaum was on a major trade route and relatively inconspicuous. Here, talk of a new "Kingdom" might be safe for a time.

God in Full Strength

Increasingly the conversation focused on that. To announce the coming of God's Kingdom was Jesus' one goal. He wanted the whole nation to hear that good news. God was coming as king: coming in full strength and power. That was the central reality in human life now.

The people in that room knew there were two kinds of power. There was the kind you saw every day in that harshly unequal world, where political leaders and great landlords kept you powerless and poor.

But the power Jesus was speaking of was for healing and full life. It was like the triumph of great harvests; it was life making a broken family whole. It was power that you shared in and rejoiced in and celebrated with all.

"Through *me*," Jesus was saying, "God's power is coming to you."

Could God come to full power in Israel through a nonentity from Nazareth? Well, perhaps Jesus was something more than that? Some people were already talking of his healings. There was the freshness and authority of his teaching in the synagogue. There was the conviction, the peace, and warmth of his personality. And, anyway, hadn't God often chosen "nonentities"?

They knew so well the great prophecies Jesus was now claiming to be fulfilled. They could recall the exultant message of victory for all of God's People:

> How wonderful it is to see a messenger
> coming across the mountains,
> bringing good news, the news of peace!
> He announces victory and says to Zion,
> "Your God is king." (Isaiah 52:7)

Not defeat and reprisals, and for many slavery in foreign lands, but instead the Rule of a God who would bring his People to all good.

But where was this power Jesus confidently claimed? In this small, bare room, in a second-rate town, with an odd collection of people from several walks of life, *could* God really be coming in his full power?

When that happened, the Romans would be thrown out—but was Jesus mustering a force to set Israel free? Another of their expectations was the purging of God's People: only the virtuous would constitute it then. But was a man who invited toll-collectors and harlots to his meals making God's People clean?

Jesus tried to bring the great Isaiah images back to their minds:

good news to the poor,
healing for the broken-hearted,
release to captives,
joy and gladness instead of grief.
(Isaiah 61:1,3)

That would be a world transformed: a new kind of creation. It would be fashioned for everyone by a God who loves. A far cry from battles and purging.

So were the images of God making his dispersed People whole: "bringing you together, like sheep returning to the fold." (Micah 2:12)

But could a subjugated people, restive for self-respect and freedom, recognize God's full coming in anything short of war?

Perhaps that evening some had begun to glimpse a deeper reality. They could recognize in Jesus compassion and healing. He had invited the "virtuous" and public sinners together to his meal. He seemed to be reaching out to them, inviting them, to help them form a new world.

Would they see him again, as he evidently wanted? Was it wise to become involved with a man who was becoming controversial? Where, in any case, were the teeth in his movement?

And yet that personality, and the strange appeal of his message. . . .

Wordlessly, he had confronted them with a fundamental decision.

Three

Healing

The streets and alleys of a deprived country are not for the squeamish. You see the physically and mentally disabled sitting or lying helpless in filth. You see them begging or scavenging for the bare essentials of life.

In the Palestine of Jesus' time there were no hospitals. There were some doctors, but only for the rich. In the small, cramped houses where most people lived, it was often impossible to keep indefinitely the violently ill.

The Gospels often show Jesus within this kind of situation. They help us reconstruct a typical healing done by him.

A Typical Healing

The people in the marketplace would be aware of the blind beggar on his usual pitch. Occasionally, his pleas penetrated their consciousness. Then, suddenly, there was a whisper that Jesus had come. Would he go over to the beggar? Would there be a cure? Would it be by black magic, as some were claiming? Or would it be a sign, as Jesus claimed, that Israel's great hopes were coming true?

Now groups and individuals were forming a crowd round Jesus. Some were looking for the sensational, some for something more.

As Jesus approached the sick person, it was obvious that he cared. He stood or squatted beside him, waiting for a response. Everything depended on the blind man's trust in Jesus. It was his trust that could work the cure, not Jesus by himself.

If you were close enough you could see Jesus' efforts to bring out the beggar's trust. He knew that mere theory about God could not make sense of misery and loss of dignity. The only thing that could do that was a sense of God's presence.

Sometimes a blind beggar could feel more involved than others in the long story of that presence. His experience of kindness from his fellow members, his use of prayers of trust and hope that had been found valid for many centuries, his sense of belonging, in spite of all, at Sabbath worship or great feasts: these could mean more to someone like him, who had nothing, than to those who were secure.

The Jews at their best had never seen religion as just theory. It was about finding God in the reality of people's lives. God was in all their everyday experience. He was also in the great forces that shape the destinies of us all. In all the failure, pain and mess, in all the achievement and joy, God was somehow bringing everything to good.

Even misery and degradation were not the same from that standpoint. Perhaps, for long periods, you could only feel the pain. But at a deeper level of consciousness you might feel upheld by God's hand.

The old cries of hope of your people could make sense to you now:

My sores stink and rot.
I am bowed down, I am crushed.
My friends and neighbors will not come near me;
even my family keeps away from me.

O Lord, you know what I long for;
you hear all my groans.

I trust in you, O Lord;
you, O Lord my God, will answer me.

Do not stay away, my God!
Help me now, O Lord my Saviour.
(Psalm 38)

Perhaps the blind beggar with Jesus mumbled some of those old-remembered words. He had heard rumors about Jesus; now he felt his presence. A look of trust began to form on that tough, gnarled face. "If you will, you can cure me, sir," he managed to say.

So the healing began. It didn't come in a flash. Jesus' healings were not instantaneous laser beams "vaporizing" illness. They were two people's joint struggle for that man or woman's wholeness: wholeness of the body, wholeness of the heart and mind.

The Gospel accounts preserve for us some short sketches of those struggles. They were written 40-60 years later, when the physical details were not the main point. But some of them let us see how strongly physical the cures were.

Curing a deaf man, Jesus "put his fingers to his ears, spat and touched his tongue." (Mark 7:33) Curing a blind man, Jesus "spat on his eyes and laid his hand upon him"; and since the cure was still incomplete, Jesus "laid his hands on his eyes again" so that he saw clearly. (Mark 8:23-25)

That was the way healings were conducted, both in Palestine and elsewhere. A healing was a huge turning around in your whole basic situation. That had to be worked out and felt in *every* part of you.

In a healing, the *whole* of you regained harmony with life's deepest forces. Through your interplay with the healer you found that you could trust those forces. The *whole* of both of you had to feel and express this pivotal discovery. Hence, smearing the body, or touching each other; hence also, great shouts and even cries of ecstasy. All these could be the means by which all aspects of you were involved.

"Demons"

Both the healer and the healed felt themselves in a struggle with the deepest layers of human evil. They believed in God: believed that the basic direction of all was good. But in illness and much else they saw a dreadful counterforce.

In some of Jesus' and others' cures, there was expelling of "demons." As Orientals, they naturally pictured this counterforce—of many kinds—as an array of personal forces. All nations then—and many still—believe the world populated by a host of "demons." The art of life was to appease and pander to them.

For a long time, the Hebrews had rejected any belief in demons. Their God controlled all: so how could there be rivals? Suffering and evil, however terrible, must somehow be "under" God.

Then Greek civilization swept over Palestine, about two centuries before Jesus. The view of evil as personalized in demons became part of the air you breathed.

So the Jews came to accept the universal belief in demons. But they held that belief in a different form from the rest. For them they were a dreaded force, but could never be paramount. Their God was supreme—he allowed demons only for his purposes. So the art of life wasn't to pander to demons. The key was God's loving call.

Cures could therefore be pictured as expelling demons. That helped one appreciate the cosmic power of evil. Jesus and those he healed shared that contemporary standpoint. He, too, might "command" evil to leave that person, treating it, like others, as a personal "demon." But, like mainstream Jews at least, he never tried to manipulate the "demon" with the "right" incantation. "Demons" were a good way for an Oriental (and others) to appreciate the destructiveness and power of evil. But they weren't the rulers of a world in which there is no God.

Offence

So the *manner* in which Jesus conducted his cures was accept-
able to those who saw them. Faith-healings took this kind of
form both in Palestine and beyond. True, the number performed
by Jesus may well have been unique: "through all antiquity no
other man is credited by so many miracles."[1] But that wouldn't,
by itself, have caused offence.

But quite quickly Jesus' cures became disturbing to the establishment.

Most other such cures were not seen by them as threatening.
When rabbis performed such cures, you had the marvel of the
healing and a boost for his reputation. When there was a healing
at one of the Greek shrines of Asclepius—like Epidaurus, "the
Greek Lourdes"—all that was threatened was the already-low
reputation of doctors.

One reason for the alarm was the *kind* of faith-healer Jesus
clearly was. He was one of those Jews who found in themselves
God's revolutionary power. God was using them, they believed,
to change the world. They were revolutionary "charismatics," out
to change the status quo. Any healings they might perform were
just a part of that work.

That Jesus was of this kind became clear in his healings on
the Sabbath. The original purpose of the Sabbath had long been
lost to view. Instead of a weekly occasion to enjoy creation, as
God's work and yours, the Sabbath had become a matter of petty
rules about levels of physical activity. But, in that occupied
country, the observance of the Sabbath was a mark of national
and religious identity. Jesus' breaking those rules undermined
their sense of religion and that identity.

The cures were as threatening to that identity as Jesus' welcoming toll-collectors and prostitutes. In both he was breaking
down barriers that the establishment believed to be indispen-
sable. Israel was a beleaguered race, and Jesus was knocking
down some of its "vital" walls.

---

1. Morton Smith, *Jesus the Magician,* San Francisco 1978, p. 109.

If Jesus' offensive practices had been no more than the behavior of a freak, that would have been scandalous, but probably not intolerable. But Jesus was presenting himself as much more than just an individual. He was claiming that through him *God* was coming in full power. In his work and in all he stood for, God was fully available. The whole direction of the world was now fundamentally changed, he said. "If you look at me objectively, that's what you can see."

Sometimes he would cry out with great joy at the nature of that change. The whole tide of evil was being decisively turned back. As an Oriental, he pictured that in the form of a grand cosmic scene. "I saw Satan falling like lightning from heaven," was his exultant cry. (Luke 10:18)

"Can't you see that is true?" he asked, to those who stood around him. "It's God's Spirit—God's creative power—that enables me to drive out demons. Surely that is proof that the Rule of God is coming to you?" (Matthew 12:28)

The way he made those claims increased his critics' sense of danger. His own role was hardly mentioned in his teaching. No views or practices were forced on your assent. There was just the quiet, strong urging to consider his actions. "Can't you see in this the Rule of God?" he asked.

This quiet insistence on evidence and this self-effacedness: these were hardly the characteristics of any kind of freak.

Added to this was the strong, rich texture of his own character. He had a sense of mission to all, yet love for all types of individuals. There was his awareness of great powers, but for others, not himself. There was his reverence for tradition, but also willingness to buck the system.

Of course, he wasn't unique in showing contradictions in his character. But in Jesus, apparent opposites didn't appear as contradictions. They seemed to show, instead, his strength and richness of character.

All this flowed from and showed forth the Rule of God he stood for. That Rule formed Jesus' one central purpose. It was in this rock-like integrity, this sense of wholeness, that the "threat" of Jesus lay.

That, however, was only the beginning of the "threat." On top of the behavior and the character, there was the factor of the crowds. In an occupied country, longing to be free, crowds could lead into riots and even spark off war.

Those who believed in Jesus' message could welcome that prospect. But from the establishment's point of view, real horror was here. For a truly pious Jew to endanger peace might have been bad enough. But Jesus wasn't a pious Jew: he ignored hallowed Laws. He did this with an unshakable sense of righteousness and widening appeal. Many pious Jews felt faced with something fundamentally wrong, unreasonable, insane, that could not be controlled. Jesus must be "possessed" by Satan. When Jesus cured the sick, he must do this through Satan's power. (Mark 3:22)

Jesus replied by pointing out the absurdity of that view. "How can Satan drive out Satan?" (Mark 3:23) A different explanation had to be found. Could they not accept the one Jesus gave?

Jesus' Explanation

Jesus' explanation was the same as for everything else he did. The course of history had changed. "The right time has come; God's Rule is near." (Mark 1:15) In that corner of the market place, or wherever a cure took place, you were seeing God's powerful coming, Israel's hope and prayer.

So, what was it like, that coming? A dazzling display of miraculous powers? A merely "religious" event, remote from our real lives?

Jesus saw it as taking place, instead, at the center of that beggar's need. It was not imposed on him: he was free to choose "yes" or "no." If he accepted God's offer of powerful coming, it transformed his whole life. Yes, it restored his health; but it also went much further. It put him in full touch with life's deepest forces. He now knew his life to be safe in God's whole loving plan.

None of this took place in a "supernatural" display. The healer and the healing looked much like any other. The beggar remained his own master. God's Rule liberated and affirmed, and was entirely human.

Today's Perspectives

Today we see Jesus' healings from our own perspectives. We may share some of our contemporaries' doubts about miracles themselves. So we need to examine the evidence about three questions: Did Jesus really heal? If so, what were those healings like? And what can they say to us today?

Did Jesus really heal?

The chief evidence for the belief that Jesus healed is, obviously, the Gospels. But weren't they written by Christians who were more interested in what Jesus meant to them—and could mean to others—than in the details of his life in Palestine? And weren't they written decades after Jesus' death?

The answer to both questions has to be "Largely, yes." It's true that the earliest Gospel, Mark, was written about 35 years after Jesus' death—though all the Gospels use material that goes back decades before that. It's also true that their writers were much more interested in the *significance* of a man who had conquered death than they were in reporting accurately the events of his life.

These facts have to be taken into account as we look at the Gospels. The writers were not "on the spot" reporters. Their aim is not to tell us exactly "how it was." They are Christians helping their community, a generation or two later, to live and die in partnership with the Jesus they had come to know and to love in their own lives and in those of others. What fired them to write was their conviction that Jesus lived in them.

They had found that in themselves and in their fellow-Christians, Jesus was making available, in different ways, the power of God ("the Spirit"). Christian life was about making that power fruitful. You had to use it in the specific context of your own problems and opportunities. So the focus had now moved from Palestine in the 20s. It was now on Christian communities, outside Palestine, in the second half of that century. These communities wanted to reflect on how Jesus could be more present to them now.

But this risen Jesus was the man who had worked and died in Palestine. What had happened in his resurrection was the outcome of the life he had led in its towns and its lanes. There people had come to know his personality and his loveableness, and there his victory over death and evil had begun to be achieved.

So in the Gospels we find in fact a *double* agenda. The main facts about Jesus' life were of fundamental importance to them. But these were to be told in such a way as to help their contemporaries deal as Christians with different situations.

When we look at the outcome of these facts in the miracle stories themselves, the results may seem startling. In every major strand of the Gospels, there is great emphasis on Jesus' healings and exorcisms. We will soon come to other reasons for believing that Jesus performed such actions. But in the great majority of these narratives, the writers are not recording actual incidents.

This was partly for the reasons we have already seen: the relevance, more than the factual details, was the important thing for the communities. Another factor was the way miracle-stories were customarily told in the Gospel writer's world. Just as in Shakespeare's time it became close to "obligatory" to write your play in five Acts, so in Greek civilization there were five accepted components of a miracle story. So in Christian communities, those telling the stories were expected to try to conform with the customary pattern. Where a component of the pattern (like praise at the end) hadn't taken place, then it seemed necessary to insert it.

By the time these stories were gathered up into the Gospels, it was often impossible to distinguish between the actual events, added parts, or invented typical stories. This did not trouble the Gospel writers. They and their readers knew that Jesus had performed such deeds. That general fact was the thing that chiefly mattered. Their concern was to emphasize that in their accounts of healings and their statements about them. But this must be done in the ways to which their (Greek) culture was accustomed.

One example of this is the healing of Bartimaeus. (Mark 10:46- 52) If the writer just wanted a typical story, why invent the Aramaic name? Besides the beggar's name, we have the place name (Jericho) and other details of life in Jesus' time. It looks like a story told in Jericho, by Bartimaeus, after Jesus' death. Even so, Mark felt free to reshape it for the purposes of his community. He wanted to emphasize that Jesus didn't only cure your body, he also called you to follow him through life. His readers were accustomed to a call-and-follow story having a certain shape. So Bartimaeus' vivid recollections of his healing are cast in that shape.

The cure of Peter's mother-in-law is one of the other stories that seems to reflect an actual healing.

Of the 20 healing narratives in the Gospels, all arise from the conviction that Jesus cured sick people, but probably as few as six recount actual cures. Although we have seen why the Gospel writers weren't chiefly interested in being "reporters" of the scenes in Jesus' life, we can still feel let down by finding the scant concern with actual events. It's true that we may suspect that our preoccupation with wanting precise facts can be at the expense of interest in the *meaning* of Jesus' cures: meaning not just for individuals, but ultimately for us all. But even then we may have some sense of unease or suspicion. If so few accounts are factual, can we be sure that Jesus healed at all?

The evidence that Jesus did heal consists of several strands. It's when we see these together that we can judge the strength of the case.

First, there is the fact that the evidence is so widespread.

The Gospel accounts are only one place that we find that evidence. There we find a massive assertion that Jesus did heal. Large portions of the Gospels describe his healing activity.

Behind the Gospels we can deduce considerably earlier Christian sources, some of which can be traced to a period at least very close to Jesus' own lifetime. In these there is also the firm conviction that Jesus healed.

Even more persuasive, perhaps, is evidence from Jesus' opponents. They were saying that it was "by Beelzebub"[2] that Jesus cast out demons. (Matthew 12:27) Christians would never have *invented* that accusation against Jesus whom they now believed to be "Son of God." Therefore, we can be sure that the charge was leveled against him. If Jesus' opponents had not believed that there was evidence that Jesus did heal, the accusation itself would, of course, have been pointless. This case is made still stronger by Jesus' story about a divided household—itself a very Palestinian-type story. (Matthew 12:25-26)

This belief by Jesus' Jewish opponents that he did practise black magic survived long after his death. We find in a Jewish writing 170 years after his death: "On the eve of the Pasch Jesus was executed . . . because he had practised (black) magic, seduced Israel and led people from the true faith."

What were those healings like?

In our reconstruction of a cure by Jesus, we assumed that his cures were faith healings. This seems clear from two facts. One is that Jesus' cures were not seen by him or by others as different from those of others—where "faith" was important. The other fact is that all the illnesses cured by him are of the kind that arise from psychotic problems. Such problems are resolved by regaining trust and inner harmony.

Of course, this claim that Jesus' cures did not differ from those of others must seem offensive to those who imagine Jesus as living a superhuman life in Palestine. That he had superhuman *power* was his chief assertion: "through my healings you should recognize in me the power or 'Rule' of God." (Matthew 12:28) But the claim of Jesus and the Gospels is that this superhuman power was working in *human* beings, operating in them in *human* ways. They saw this as true of Jesus, as well as of his followers.

It was present in deeply human things like healings and supper parties; in refusing to hate or give in; in love, tolerance and compassion; in companionship and courage: all in the everyday

---

2. A Galilean name for a demon, not necessarily the chief demon.

context of that particular time and place. It is because of the four-square *humanness* of the whole Jesus story that we need to sift, very honestly, the evidence about the healings. Some will prefer a Jesus whose actions are somehow "above" objective scrutiny. But that amounts to denying incarnation.

The point of Jesus' life was God-made-flesh, incarnation. In such things as Jesus' "ordinary" healings, God was entering our human situation and our future with climactic fullness.

All these factors have led an outstanding Scripture scholar to write about Jesus' healings that "the modern reader of the Bible can attribute Jesus' healings and exorcisms to the natural radiance of his personality: an explanation that becomes increasingly probable in the light of modern psychosomatic medicine."[3]

The apparently conflicting factor is one of the narratives of Jesus' exorcisms. We have seen that most of the narrative of Jesus' healings and exorcisms is probably not recording actual cures.

The same can also be true of the accounts of Jesus curing epilepsy. When we apply the generally-agreed yardsticks for deciding when we *do* have an actual healing in front of us, only one of them falls into this category.[4] There, Jesus exorcises an epileptic boy.

Two doctors have recently stressed how full and accurate is the account we get from the three Gospel accounts of the main stages of epilepsy. The same is true of the possible results of the disease: "The danger to life and limb from falling into the fire or into water are well-documented features of epilepsy."[5]

Some kinds of epilepsy are of unknown causes; but fits can occur as a result of psychosomatic disorders. This actual case,

---

3. Rudolph Pesch, *Theologische Quartalschrift*, 1972, p. 205.

4. Matthew 17:14-21

5. Dr. J. Keir Howard, Wellington Clinical School of Medicine (3) (*Expository Times* 1985 Vol. 96, no. 4, p. 107). The other doctor is Dr. John Wilkinson (in his book, *Health and Healing: Studies in New Testament Principles and Practice*, Edinburgh 1980, pp. 61-69). My niece, Dr. Nichola Beck, kindly discussed this chapter with me.

and the others it may represent, could therefore have been cured by Jesus in the way we have seen.

Four

Helping Friends with Problems

What Jesus was doing could not long remain private. You might be in the marketplace or in a house when he cured a sick person. You saw him breaking the "rules" of religious teaching by teaching in the streets. Sooner or later you heard of the meals he often had.

What particularly set people talking was: *Where is all this leading?* There was immense uncertainty about Jesus' intentions. His refusal to spell them out increased both the hopes and the fears. Was he planning, with his followers, armed struggle against the Romans? Would he attempt, in the name of God, to get their armies out?

There were unmistakable indications that that might be the case. Jesus was proclaiming: "Now God is coming to rule." That brought back strong memories of Judas of Galilee, the great Jewish rebel. It was only a generation ago that he had demanded revolt against the Romans because "only God is ruler." Judas had been as fearless as Jesus. Like Jesus, too, he had seemed to some to be Messiah.

Judas was called by a contemporary "a contentious scribe from Galilee." He had "caused the Jews to go wild and to revolt against the Romans." Would this other "contentious" teacher take the same course?

Some of the townsfolk were noticing another similarity. Jesus' followers were quite different from those of the rabbis. Becoming a disciple of a rabbi was like joining a respectable law firm. It was likely to bring a peaceful, secure existence, and social advancement.

But they knew that there was also another kind of "following." You left home and family, job and security, because total involvement was demanded by the task in hand.

In a country like the Jews', where family was deeply reverenced, only national emergency could justify such a demand. When it was being made, crisis was in the air.

Judas and other rebels had made those demands. Now Jesus was making them to his closest followers. He was forming a group around himself who gave up everything.

So, *what was the emergency that this group was meant to tackle?* "Through me," Jesus was saying, "God is becoming ruler." He was announcing a new world, but not vaguely, in the future. The emergency was in your midst; the opportunity was now.

Surely that opportunity must consist of getting the Romans out? His likeness to Judas fuelled that expectation. There was the excitement of standing on the brink of a great future. Gone would be the indignity of subjection to another people. Gone the taxes that brought many to bankruptcy and even slavery. They would have their own land, to love and to cherish. They would be able to boast, to all the world, of being God's favored People.

Dreams of such huge appeal can spread like forest fires. The yearning for their realization can sweep all else before it. Some people in Capharnaum were *certain* of Jesus' aim. He *must* be God's Messiah, to set his People free.

Others eagerly looked for evidence that indeed that was his goal. If only they could be certain that the dawn was near. It was galling to find facts that cast doubt on their great hope.

Doubts

Was Jesus offering the kind of leadership the true Messiah must show? He was making no attempt to summon the crowds to war. It wasn't weakness or half-heartedness—he was never accused of fear. But he was failing to focus on achieving his aims by war.

This disappointment was compounded by other impressions. A man like Judas of Galilee had shown a burning consciousness of his "charisma" of leadership. He stirred great crowds with his personal appeal. "You are confronted, at last, with God's Messiah sent to rescue you," Judas had seemed to be saying. "The future you have so longed for is now within your grasp. At this moment of destiny, who can fail to follow?"

When would they hear from *Jesus* such impassioned pleas? If he was bringing in God's rule, he must be the Messiah. Surely, consciousness of his own role must stir him to public challenge?

Leadership with a Difference

Some were open to the possibility of a different kind of leadership. They could see that Jesus seemed conscious of himself, but in a vastly different way. In his meals and in his stories, in his actions and his prayers, his overwhelming consciousness was less of himself than of God.

The God he was conscious of was not an inhabitant of a "higher world" reached by rite and prayer. For him, God was present at the center of the action. As Father, he was transforming the whole human situation. This transformation was now happening through Jesus, and all who joined him. Those close to him sometimes felt caught up in the splendor of that consciousness. Somehow they felt involved in the birth of that new world.

In Jesus' suppers, for example, they felt the strength of his emotions when his stories spoke of growth and harvest. They knew that this group round the table would be no match for the Roman troops. Even the small garrison in Capharnaum would treat a threat from them with scorn. Yet from this tiny "mustard seed" a great bush would come. This tiny, despised force would "leaven" the whole batch.

Most moving of all was the tone of these stories. When he described the huge yield ("even a hundredfold"), there was enthusiasm, joy and utter assurance.

But Jesus wasn't like a self-made man, revelling in his achievement. He wasn't like a miser counting his fields or cattle, or fondling his store of gold. What filled him with such emotions wasn't *his* work but God's! In it he knew the Father, loving and powerful. The Father was ruler now. His "kingship" would come. All that was human here would somehow come to good. Freedom would remain; and great evils would be done. But all was now moving towards harvest-time.

But it would be *God's* harvest, not his. It would be so much more than the achievement of any human individual. It would be the coming to open power of the one who guides and spans all.

It was his openness to that God that was Jesus' main quality: openness to the force at the center of all that is.

Disciples

You could see that in his relationship to his followers. Rebels like Judas of Galilee claimed titles; Jesus claimed none. Rabbis were served by their pupils; Jesus insisted on serving all. A rabbi's pupil must imitate his master; Jesus pointed only to involvement in the coming of God's kingship.

Even the demand to give up everything was not for its own sake. Still less was it the dismal denial of the world's essential goodness that others would later make it. It came simply from his reading of the current situation. God's kingship was coming now. The struggle was huge and urgent. At this time of crisis, only total effort would suffice. He himself had had to sacrifice everything for this overriding need. Those who accepted his call to be close partners must respond, realistically, to the needs of the same role.

It was typical of Jesus that he made no "law" about this. He showed no interest in a system—only in response to reality. To attempt to be his closest partner and not to give up everything was to try to live a contradiction in the present crisis.

He did not ask everyone to join him so closely. He invited a few to do that; the rest joined to the extent they could. Just as his teaching invited you to mature decision, his way of being a leader had the same goal. His "discovery," after all, was God's power in all his *different* people. How absurd to act as if its ways could be uniform!

So he took people as they were, in all their diversity. Unlike the rabbis, he would speak to the crowds. He flouted convention and preached in the streets. The contemptuous mutterings of the town "establishment" had to be ignored.

If you did decide to join him, you followed your own route. You yourself decided the level of your involvement.

All you were asked to do was to open yourself to the actual situation. You remembered God's long presence with his People and his promise to come fully. You saw the power in Jesus, his personality and his message. Would you let all that change your perceptions and attitudes?

If your way of life was immoral, would you let God move you from that? If you were proud or selfish, would you be drawn to Jesus' ways? Above all, would you let yourself be fired by a conviction that through this man God's People were becoming whole again—the people you saw before you, sinners and all?

Jesus was claiming that it was becoming whole again—on a tiny scale, but momentously. A People was being formed to become "a light for the whole world."

A Hardening Opposition

It was difficult to change old attitudes and accept such massive claims. Respected people in the town were saying that he was nothing but a fraud. They were pointing to evidence that could not be denied.

Didn't religious teaching consist of application of the Law? Learned argument must proceed from principle and precedent. The scribes who taught in that way had long been highly regarded.

At first, the scribes had been impressed by Jesus' teaching in the synagogue. They had been glad to let him preach, as any layman could.

But soon there came a shift in official policy. Jesus' teaching was not based on that firm foundation. It was not deduced from the Law by careful, learned argument. Yes, it was popular with the crowds—but in these tense, expectant times they would follow almost anyone. Yes, his disciples had given up everything—but so did followers of rebels set on civil war. Since Jesus' teaching was not based on Law, it must be seduction of the masses.

Respectable opinion hardened: Jesus was dangerous and a seducer. Anyone following him was letting God's People down.

"Teaching With Authority"

But some of Jesus' friends were beginning to draw the opposite conclusion. Yes, it was difficult to accept a form of teaching so different from the one they knew. In normal circumstances they would probably have sided with the scribes. But there was something in Jesus' teaching that drew them as nothing had before.

One of the most obvious things about it was that it was not borrowed from others. He taught with the "authority" of one who speaks from first-hand experience. There was no "I think," or "This scholar says," or "You will find in this book."

There was the complete authority, for example, with which he had called his disciples. And there was the conviction with which he proclaimed as *the* Good News that God's kingship was now.

Teachers' great interest in their message and their role can weaken their response to other people; and the truths in their message can blind them to other truths. They can become rigid or fanatical, and cruel with any deviants.

At Jesus' meals, particularly, you saw something entirely different. There was the smile and warm welcome for the toll-collector and the prostitute.

He was "for" them as they were: inviting them into his family; calling them to accept in their lives the power of God they had begun to glimpse.

Not that he steamrollered his "liberal" policy over the other people there. He knew their feelings, and what prompted them; and he would try to help them through them.

He did not seek to lead either "side" with the bludgeon of a statement: "You are simply wrong. You must immediately accept my ways." Instead he told them stories, asked them to view for themselves bits of life:

> What do you think about this imaginary situation? What attitudes do you take to it? Consider whether that situation has parallels with my work among you. Could the attitudes you take to this bit of fiction be just as applicable to what you are seeing me do?"

So despite the authoritativeness of his teaching, he always respected your human dignity. He took you where you were—with your own attitudes and situation. It was in human beings, not in ciphers, that God's kingship was coming.

He tried to show how important that was to him in several of those stories. It wasn't that sensitiveness to your individuality just happened to attract him. In fact, what interested him wasn't primarily *his own* decisions at all. The whole point of Jesus' life was to show the ways of *God*. In all he was and in all he did, that was his only role. God's way was to take account of the individual persons there. Therefore it was also Jesus' way.

So here was no fanatic, with a rigidly pre-set mind. Determination there was; and absolute conviction. He *knew* with all his mind and heart that God was coming fully through him. But he could smile at the "improbability," even "absurdity" of God's ways—yes, indeed, he was "mustard seed" or "leaven" (both a kind of dirty word). At best, the time and shape of that coming he only partly knew. His conviction did not close him to the complexities of the ordinary human situation—or even to the limitations of his own very human life.

With this lack of fanaticism went his lack of self-assertion—amazing in someone making such massive claims. He knew there was tangible anger that he would not claim the Messiah title. People saw him speak and act with the assurance of an intimate "insider". He acted as one who *knows* his closeness to the mind of God. In spite of all that, he would not claim a title. He refused to focus what was happening on an individual's "cause". His only interest was in *God's* coming to birth in people.

Jesus and the Outcasts

But how could God be coming fully through a person who was inviting moral scum to be part of his religious family?

As Jesus looked around the table, he could read that doubt in his friends' eyes. The feelings of contempt in those outside could easily be imagined.

Typically, he tackled the question with a story. But his answer was wider than the story itself. His stories seldom tried to prove things: they helped you draw right conclusions from your own experience. And his friends' experience of Jesus and the outcasts had begun some time ago. It was on that experience that his story would partly build.

His treatment of them this evening had been similar to what they had seen him do before. He had welcomed them to his house, shown sympathy and friendship. He had tried to make them feel at home, and bring them into his circle.

Some found it difficult to feel entirely unmoved by what this clearly meant to the outcasts. From despised outsiders, they had become honored friends. Their happiness and gratitude shone in their faces.

In quiet, discreet ways, Jesus had been encouraging his friends to join in his welcome to the outcasts. Grudgingly and slightly, a few of them complied. Jesus knew that deeply-held beliefs do not normally change quickly.

He was trying to help them build on these small beginnings. He wanted them to discover that his own treatment of these outcasts was the only one possible. To try to achieve all that, he told them a story.

Typically, he began the story by appealing to their own mature judgement. Not "I'm telling you: you must accept this," but "In the light of your own experience, how does this look to you?"

His story asked them to begin with their experience of shepherds. "Suppose you had a flock of a hundred sheep and had the misfortune of losing one of them. Would you not leave the 99 in that desolate hill country and go after the lost sheep until you found it?"

Of course, they knew all about the realities of that profession. They could put themselves in the situation of a shepherd who lost one of his flock.

The fact that losing sheep was easy would not help his situation. Thieves, wild animals, and the rough terrain were familiar enough hazards. But the most likely explanation, in an employer's mind, would be the dishonesty of the shepherd. What could be easier in the remote pastures where sheep had to graze than to sell a sheep or two and pretend it had been lost? A shepherd with a reputation for such dishonesty would be likely to be unemployable. Utter poverty, or slavery, would be his future now.

So Jesus could count on his guests agreeing with the drift of his story. *Of course* any shepherd would leave the 99 (in the hands of his mates) "and go after the lost sheep until he finds it."

They would equally go along with the rest of the story. Naturally he "rejoiced" when he found the lost sheep. Since a lost sheep will lie down helplessly and refuse to budge, he would have to carry on his shoulders its cumbersome, huge weight. But the relief of the finding made the burden seem light.

By the time he reached the village, his colleagues would have driven the rest of the flock back there for safety at night. He wants all his neighbors to join in celebrating the find. A big loss

to him would have been in some degree a loss to them, too.[1]
Jesus' listeners could picture them joining in the fun.

So Jesus' story described a chain of events they could readily
understand. They could enter into the feelings of all those involved. They recognized from this and his other stories his grasp
of human life. Even for a travelling builder, as he had been, his
range of interest was extraordinary. Now that he was proclaiming God's rule, it had become no less.

Was he suggesting that God's life and human life were not
separate compartments? You could discover it in a shepherd's
experience or in a mustard seed, in a meal or a catch of fish. You
met its thrust and movement everywhere, if you opened your
eyes.

That dimension could more easily be found here through an
unmistakable allusion. A shepherd seeking out the lost brought
echoes of one of the Bible's greatest promises:

> I am going to look after my flock myself.
> I shall rescue them from wherever they have been,
>   scattered during the mist and the darkness . . .
> I shall look for the lost one, bring back the strong,
>   bandage the wounded and make the weak strong.
> (Ezekiel 34:11-16)

That was *God's* promise to his People: he would pasture them
like a flock. He would make them whole again. "What joy and
what beauty would be theirs!" (Zechariah 9:17)

So Jesus was explaining *his* actions by reminding them what
God would do! It was all right for him to reach out to the "lost,"
because God had promised to do that when the climax came.

The sheer effrontery of that claim sent waves round the room.
This baffling man from Nazareth—so ordinary, yet so unique:
should you laugh or be angry at his monstrous claims? Or was it
thinkable that you should bow before the full presence of God?

There were some things about that evening that could incline
you towards that second choice. Jesus' story had described a

---

1. It seems that there was a kind of informal mutual insurance system among
villagers.

reaching out to the "lost" as a joy in which all shared. That evening, it was difficult to feel *no* sense of shared joy. Only the rigidly self-righteous could remain unmoved at the looks of gratitude and relief on the faces of the outcasts. Up to then, they had felt condemned to the "mist and darkness" of general contempt. Perhaps their own *self*-contempt was the most difficult to bear. Now they were welcomed by a person whose whole presence spoke of peace.

As the evening had gone on, some may have begun to behave like Jesus. Jesus' story was his invitation to develop further what these had perhaps already begun. It conjured up God's tenderness and concern: his care and protection for the weak. "That's not a pious theory in a book. It's now happening through me, and through you so far as you agree to become my 'family.' You are experiencing, with me, what it's like now that God rules. My story is an invitation, an opportunity, to build with confidence on our joy."

When Jesus had finished his story, there was a long pause. Each guest was trying to cope with a conflict of beliefs and emotions.

For centuries, their people had known God as their shepherd, especially in times of need. Their psalmist had sung of that in a song they still loved. It told of how God had responded to their human needs with care and tenderness, both when they had been slaves in Egypt and ever since.

> The Lord is my shepherd
> I have everything I need. (Psalm 23:1)

Food and water, shelter and tending: the Lord as shepherd provides them all in that song. Not as a remote state governor, but as someone immediately by your side: "I will not be afraid, Lord, for you are with me," was the psalmist's confident cry.

The song could not stop at simply evoking so good a world. The singer had to "get inside" such goodness, by celebrating it with this Shepherd and with others. Just like Jesus and his friends that evening, in this Capharnaum house, the psalmist describes his meal of thanksgiving: an intimate celebration shared with each other and their Lord. Like Jesus this evening, the Lord had "prepared a meal" of thanks in his honor. "My cup (my life) is full," the guests sang, "of goodness and joy."

The psalmist sang of the reason: God's "goodness and loving kindness." That wasn't a random choice of one of God's many qualities. Any Jew knew that all history turned on "goodness and loving kindness" being the central characteristic of God.

Right at the beginning of the story, God had been discovered by Moses as "a God of tender kindness and compassion." (Exodus 34:6) The whole thrust of his relationship with his People was his promise to show them that. Not as a patronizing handout, but in a relationship at least as intimate as a young man with his intended bride:

> With tender kindness and love,
> I will betroth you to myself.
> And you will come to know me. (Hosea 2:21)

Yes, Jesus' guests knew all that. They had sung that psalm all their lives. But it was one thing to take satisfaction from your religious beliefs, and another thing to find them being enacted in the situation you were involved in. What more tangible enactment could there be than in that evening's events? Your beliefs coming "to earth" in such tangible, human form can, of course, be a blinding insight into the closeness of God's presence. But it was so counter to the ways of thought of many of those present that feelings of doubt and dismay were likely to be the strongest.

God "seeking out the lost" was fine as a vague religious picture; but when that seeking was through someone you knew, and when the "lost" were people whose moral lives made you squirm: then God's message easily seemed incredible.

Will the Family Become Whole Again?

On that evening, or another, Jesus tried again. This time as well he worked by means of a story. The story was devised to help his listeners reflect on key experiences they themselves had had, and on their People's long experience of God over more than 10 centuries.

The story of The Prodigal Son (Luke 15:11-32) began with a deceptive kind of ordinariness. It was normal for a younger son to raise some money and seek his living elsewhere—only 1/8 of the Jewish population then lived in Palestine. True, the way he makes the request ("sell up part of the estate") shows him implying that his father was as good as dead, so that Jesus' listeners would have expected an angry refusal. But the father, indulgently, lets the boy have his way, and the son goes off to another land.

Jesus had begun his story by saying that "A man had two sons." His story, so far, has shown that this family had now broken up. The younger son had deeply offended his father. In a foreign land, he was soon reduced to feeding pigs—an activity the Jews despised.

In his wretchedness, he repents. He will ask his father for forgiveness and try to earn back his favor.

Jesus' listeners could easily imagine the kind of reception he had receive. He had broken up an estate; he had insulted his father; he had been living a life contemptible to Jews. As he approached the village, groups would form as if by instinct. There would be loud shouting—perhaps violence. He had be given a rough time.

In fact, the predictable doesn't get a chance to happen. "While he was a long way off, his father saw him and was moved with compassion."

With that statement about compassion, the story becomes a completely different thing. Up to now it had been a not-unusual story about the breakup of a family. But the word "compassion" announced: "I'm now speaking about God." So typical of God did Jews think compassion to be that the word was kept, almost exclusively, as a word about God.

There had been Moses' discovery of "a God of tenderness and compassion." (Exodus 34:6) Then the centuries had gone by, tumultuous and testing. But at the center there had always been the same God Moses found:

> With tender kindness I have compassion for you.
> The mountains may depart,

the hills be shaken,
but my tender kindness for you will never be shaken,
and my covenant of peace will never be shaken,
says God, the compassionate. (Isaiah 54:8,10)

In spite of the much higher level it had now assumed, the story, like the Shepherd one, remains utterly human. An elderly man of position was then expected to walk in a stately manner. The father rushed towards his son, ignoring decorum and the hostile "reception committee." He hugs his son, kisses him tenderly, is almost overcome with delight. His son's plea for forgiveness he brushes aside unheard. He is too impatient to honor him to hear talk of that. The family is now whole again; all must share in that joy. *All* must join in the celebrations—the "fattened calf" would feed a whole village.

Although Jesus had not yet finished his story, waves of conflicting feelings were again going round the room. What on earth was he suggesting through this story as a reply to their questions? A "lost" sinner returned. Repentance and earning brushed aside as secondary. Compassion and the family becoming whole again the only things that counted. Was this Jesus' excuse for welcoming at his table these notorious sinners?

How could such an excuse hold any water when claimed by this man? The story, and the excuse, hinged on *God's* compassion, and *God's* wanting his family to be whole. But the questions being asked round this table, and outside in Capharnaum, were not about God's actions but about Jesus'. Those in fact were the questions that had prompted the story. How could a story evoking God give any answer to them—unless the unthinkable were true?

So the same problem was arising as with the shepherd story: Who did Jesus think he was?

Perhaps Jesus paused before starting the second half. Glances were exchanged round the table. Some comments were murmured. Several wrestled quietly in their minds with what he might be suggesting, as they sipped their wine.

The second half quickly made clear that the family was not in fact yet whole again. The elder son could not tolerate a wrongdoer being received back until he had earned back favor. Until that had been done, the person was outside the family. He refused, for that reason, to join in the party, or to call the man "brother."

Perhaps a scribe or two round Jesus' table looked offended or ill-at-ease. Their problem with Jesus welcoming toll-collectors and prostitutes was entirely a problem about earning. If these sinners had their welcome by repentance, the scribes would have been glad to welcome them. Jesus was saying that God's compassion came first. First, the experience of God in his kindness; after that, repentance as a response. Such experience, he was claiming, was now available through him. It followed that his meals with outcasts shouldn't really be a problem. They offered to everyone the experience of God we all crave: a God more "on our side" and more close to us than we ourselves can ever be. Everything now hinged on people opening their minds and hearts to that. "Will you really be like this elder brother," he was asking them, "and refuse to share in the joy of what you can see me bring?"

Jesus' story, then, offered an answer to the Jewish leaders. He knew that the rancor of some of the scribes towards him was increasing every day. But he had no hatred towards them, as the tailpiece of his story shows.

Tailpiece

The elder son's refusal to join in the father's party was, by Oriental standards, a very great insult—a queen had been executed for a similar insult to her husband. But the father in Jesus' story does not punish or become enraged. With respect, and even affection, he reminds his rebel son of the facts. "My son, you are with me always, and all I have is yours. But it was only right we should celebrate. Your *brother* here was dead and has come to life; your brother was lost and is found."

The elder son's insults are ignored; his concern about earning forgiveness is not dismissed but put into a new perspective. That perspective is family. "Aren't I your father, warm and generous? And isn't he your brother? Doesn't all that is deepest in us demand that we become family once more?"

It was a touchingly respectful plea to Jesus' critics and enemies. Some of them were trying to destroy what Jesus valued much more than his life. This was all his reply: a door wistfully left open.

Five

This Jesus

It was impossible to be unaware of the gathering clouds. Synagogues were increasingly barring Jesus from teaching. The suspicions of the authorities were more pronounced every week. The crowds were becoming disillusioned as Jesus failed to declare himself Messiah.

In a country that has endured much, tough questions get asked. What, after all, was there to Jesus? He had no base, no position, no clear system of teaching. He had a following of a sort—but the crowds were fickle—and dangerous. Even Jesus' closest friends shared the common frustration. They longed for some "action," when God's Kingship would "really" come.

But they also experienced Jesus at a different level of their personalities. This part of their experience might be difficult to square with the other. Until the two could be reconciled, great uncertainty must remain.

They were people largely like ourselves. They knew they had actual and potential strengths and their share of human weaknesses. They had to cope with their individual selves, and a whole range of people. And since day followed day, and life did not endure, they had to ask the questions sometimes about where all they valued was going.

It was in this central area of all our lives that his followers found what they had never known before. It wasn't a clear-cut understanding, from which firm policies could be deduced. It stayed incomplete, "in the air," so that your feelings could change. But it was like coming home after a long captivity and unexpectedly finding your loved ones there. You knew that your life had now somehow moved to a different level. The practical consequences would have to be tackled after.

Of course, people took different tracks on their discovery of Jesus. The initial impetus could come from his response to individuals. It didn't matter who you were—there were no "admission requirements." You might be a disgusting beggar, or a highly-respected teacher. Jesus took you for what you were, offering you his friendship and service.

For a would-be national leader, such a policy was clearly suicide. Like John the Baptist, Jesus longed for his whole nation to hear his message. This indiscriminate acceptance would alienate radically the country's respected religious guides. Jesus was jeopardizing the goal he so passionately wanted. But he clearly believed that this policy had nevertheless to be embraced. Standing with and for all in love was the message itself. Sacrifice that, and his work had no purpose.

You didn't see the toll-collectors and sick beggars received grudgingly like second-class citizens. There was compassion and respect, and the loving intimacy of the meals. Jesus positively flaunted his treating the "last" as an equal "first".

It was so different from anything they had seen: this total responsiveness. The novelty forced you to ask what lay behind it. Answers sometimes came. It might be at a meal, when you looked into his eyes. It might be after a long evening with him, as you walked home alone. In intimate or calm moments, you might *understand* what you had merely seen. You gained some degree of insight into what Jesus could mean.

What fired him was God. Perhaps for months you had seen that. You heard that in his prayer—just the way he said "Father." He didn't see the Father as a cloak, or a guarantee, of a set of abstract principles. He was experiencing God coming as a powerful ruler to bring humanity to full fruitfulness.

That was visible, as well, in his care for the poor and sick. There was no "Look at *my* great powers and do what *I* say," but "the *Lord* has filled me with his spirit to bring good news to the poor and heal the broken-hearted." The focus was on *God*, coming to heal humankind.

Then memories of his stories began to lead you further. You thought of that happy shepherd, or of the younger brother received back. You remembered the overtones that this was *God's* kind of action. In Jesus you seemed to be seeing God's coming in love to bring all to joy and fulfillment.

Such thoughts could bring great peace. At the center of all life was a compassionate, healing God. The God Jesus knew was no benevolent, aloof potentate. He could be seen in a true-to-life shepherd, or a most undignified kind of father. He could be seen in a Jesus of Nazareth who had no position and no home. God was reaching out, available somehow in this man—or this man and his family. God seemed to want this presence *shared*. You were "family"; God was Father; he knew you in your need and worth. He was summoning you to celebrate that he was bringing all to good.

You were gaining an insight into Jesus' consciousness of God and of women and men he clearly loved. Religions have a long, sad history of making belief in God involve a belittlement of human dignity. Jesus' actions and his stories insisted on full value to both.

Perhaps your discovery of Jesus, so far, had stopped at these general impressions. It was his stories that could lead you further in your journey. They brought you closer to understanding your relationship with him.

There was the story, for example, of the master who tossed to three servants an equal part of his possessions. He didn't supervise them (he left home); and he left no instructions. They had just themselves, this source of income, and the responsibility that brought.

It's these facts about themselves—not the master—that demand a true response. When the master returns and praises the servants who showed responsibility, he's not imposing his own views but expression the obvious implications of those facts.

It's the same, Jesus said, with God's coming as King. He's not an arbitrary ruler with a set of strange requirements. He's not an anxious overseer, crimping our freedom. At the heart of the relationship is his central gift to us: our power to be fruitful. God's Rule happens in me when I use his gift as a responsible, free person.

His audience would have recognized that, from a business standpoint, the story was daft. What kind of investor would entrust his or her possessions to agents *equally*, with no concern for greater or lesser aptitude?

The daftness served to bring out his point that in God's Rule, unlike the business world, each has a full share. I may have few abilities; heredity, or other circumstances, may make me heavily disadvantaged. Jesus was, after all, no stranger to people living in apparently hopeless situations.[1] But in my own way, I'll be given the same share as all; whether my "yield" is five-fold or ten-fold, I'll be given the same reward.[2]

The one imperative was to let God's Kingship come to fruit in you: to accept life and creativity as a loving gift to be freely used. If you refused, there wouldn't be punishment as an expression of arbitrary laws or anger.[3] You would be what you had freely decided: a person without real fruit. "If you refuse to love," John said much later, "you must remain dead." (1 John 3:15)

So God becoming King doesn't lessen our importance. It consists, instead, of our realizing our full selves. In the Good Samaritan story, that was further developed.

The story started with the question: Who is my neighbor? For centuries, the Jews had known that they must "love their neighbor as themselves." (Leviticus 19:18) The practical question became: Who must I include in that category? Family; compatriots; but after that, who else?

The story starts by placing us in the situation of a beaten-up man. He's lying by the Jericho-Jerusalem road, naked and half-

---

1. Particularly prostitutes
2. In the original parable, the two "good" servants received the same reward.
3. In the original parable, there was much less emphasis on punishment.

dead. It could happen to anyone on that steep, winding road, with wild country on either side. Jesus' listeners could easily feel themselves in that man's situation, desperate for some help.

Footsteps are heard. A priest is approaching. "Will he stop and tend my wounds and get me help before it's too late?" Instead, the wounded man heard the footsteps trail away into the distance.

Now a Temple servant came down the road. His period of duty over, like the priest he was returning home. Surely he would give help to his badly-wounded fellow-countryman? But his footsteps, too, faded into the distance.

Jesus' listeners knew that in a folk-tale the third character provides the contrast. They were expecting the story somehow to turn round. At the hinge moment Jesus, without warning, drops in two explosive words: "a *Samaritan* stops to help"; he did this "because he felt *compassion*."

The Samaritans were pariahs. For deeply religious reasons, they had been despised and hated for six centuries. The animosity had not dulled from either side of the divide. In Jesus' youth, the Samaritans had defiled the Temple during Passover by strewing human bones around it.

But this archetypal enemy helped the wounded man. Jesus seldom descends to details in his stories; but there he lists all the help the Samaritan gave. A badly-wounded person's needs are various: medicine, transport, care, food and rest. The Samaritan responds to that man in his *whole* human reality. That was the point Jesus wished to make.

A Samaritan did that; and he did it from "compassion." As in the Prodigal Son story, God's "signature tune" word is heard. There sang in Jesus' audience's ears the Isaian hymn to God's tender kindness and rock-like fidelity. But this God-type behavior was being attributed to such a hated race!

As his audience was coping, as best they could, with this blackguard-made-hero, Jesus quickly and incisively asked them a question: "Which of these three became a neighbor to that man?"

There was no need, of course, to record any answers. Answers, in any case, weren't really Jesus' point. The story had made the audience *experience* what they really meant by neighborliness, when "religious" issues had been put aside and they responded to another humanly.

They knew it needn't have been a Samaritan, or on the Jerusalem-Jericho road. So, of course, do we. I think of my friend John coming home late from his exacting work, night after night, knowing that his alcoholic wife would probably be drunk, yet treating her with care, compassion and gentleness. All kinds of images of being deeply human quickly come before us: gentle, strong faces; the understanding smile; the soothing kiss; the atmosphere that can be created in a hospice; the refusal to show disappointment when your ambitions for your child have been completely crushed.

Jesus was not just teaching morality: offering an "improving story." His business was to invite all into sharing God's Kingship. You could no longer be at the center, looking down, graciously awarding to some the category of "neighbor." You had to be like God, letting humanity's needs "master" you. Not "Who is my neighbor?" but "How can I best be neighborly?" In your practical compassion you found God coming in power—and your full self.

Six

Jesus' Aim

A full life, we often realize, consists of several threads.

We meet a person who works for the deprived—but neglects spouse or children; or someone who lives for the family, but ignores the needs of neighbors. One person lives for the present—but makes no provision for the future. Another has high ambitions for the future, but is unable to enjoy the present.

Work and play, us and them, now and the future: all are essential elements to any full life. Being fully human involves responding in some degree to them all. In that common insight lies the key to understanding what Jesus was trying to do.

The Individuals in Front of Him

Jesus showed solidarity with many threads of people's *immediate experience*.[1] His care for the individuals around him was so

---

1. What about the experience of being married? Some scholars say that St. Paul must have been married—as any Jewish male would have been expected to be. Either Paul's wife would have died, or they would have been obliged to separate because of Paul's new vocation. The same factors (which do not make a proof) may be applicable to Jesus.

obvious that it was provoking angry resentment. You saw the close friendships, especially in the meals. There was the teaching through stories that respected your freedom, and the compassion and help for those he saw in need.

His care wasn't experienced as an aloof kind of benevolence. There was obvious involvement in the lives of those he met. With a blind beggar he shared in the struggle for faith and wholeness. He sided publicly with social scum, at great risk to his work. And the greatest proof of his involvement was the depth of his love. The God whose presence he proclaimed was profoundly involved, therefore, in people's immediate pains and joys.

Wider Dimensions

Equally evident was his involvement in the *wider dimensions* of our lives. When Jesus said, "Come to dinner" to a toll-collector, it was more than a one-shot act of kindness. When he healed a sick person, you saw more than his overcoming this individual's illness.

In his stories explaining his meals, he talked of a family coming together again. He recalled the promise that the scattered "flock" of Israel would become whole. His listeners knew that he was "placing" his acts of kindness and healing in a wider, long-term context. Not just the life of that individual, but *all* human life had changed.

Today we can largely forget, for long periods, the wider dimensions of our lives. It's possible to see no further than the daily routine of our job and our own circle of friends. Most other people, and the future, can be little more than vague shadows.

Then something like a famine, or an air crash, extends our horizons. At least for a time, we feel our kinship with people perhaps far beyond our circle. We ask questions about *the purpose* and *the outcome* of what is happening; we ask what part *we* want to play, and the importance of that for us. Human experience, we then see, is more than routine punctuated by sporadic "significant" moments. We're all involved in a common story; and to be human is to take some part.

What was so moving to Jesus' friends was seeing in him *the whole spectrum* of what it is to be fully human. He met immediate needs with love and courage. But this was strengthened and developed by his wider vision.

So the friendship without barriers that you saw in him was *God coming to rule in the world as King.* His work in Palestine wasn't a one-shot life of exceptional kindness: it was *the coming of the triumphant harvest.* Those healings of the sick weren't just lucky breaks for a limited number of sick people: they were *"Satan falling like lightning from heaven."* (Luke 10:18)

All human destiny was changed. That was the unmistakable message of such images. Everything Jesus did reinforced your individual importance, whoever you might be. But you had to leave the comfortable cocoon of self, group and routine and face objectively and boldly the questions of purpose and outcome. That, for Jesus, was what the coming of God meant. It wasn't escaping from the world, but embracing it in true love.

"This Is the New Cabinet"

The climax of this embrace came in Jesus' boldest action. From a 20th-century perspective, his appointing the Twelve could seem of no great importance. But to his contemporaries it was like a Scottish Nationalist or a Native American claiming to have set up a rival administration in Edinburgh or Washington. It said, "The old order has now gone. A completely new one is here. This isn't rhetoric or dream: I have now launched it publicly."

To any Jew of Jesus' time, that claim was unmistakable. They believed that when 12 leaders were again instituted, a new world would have come. This conviction had arisen from more than a thousand years of national struggle. Flawed and fitful that long process had been—and still was in Jesus' time. But Jesus could use it to make intelligible what he believed was happening through him. Again he was building on their central experience and insights, and taking them to their limits.

That experience had partly been the common one of wanting to survive as a nation. Without national unity, you would have no chance against the frequent wars and invasions. And national unity enabled all to share in a sense of common identity, security and pride. Modern team supporters know how much shared achievement and spirit can mean.

One of the things that evoked this experience of being a whole and united nation had, for centuries, been the symbol of 12 leaders. At the grandest period in their long history, there had been 12 tribes. They could never forget the prestige and power that had been theirs under King David and King Solomon. Then in 722., B.C.E. the kingdom had broken up. The earlier greatness had never quite returned. But one day, prophets promised, God's servant would "restore the (twelve) tribes of Israel." (Isaiah 49:6) "Fortunate are those who live to see (that) come." (Sirach 48:11)

In the seven centuries since the original promise, new insights had been won. They had come from a confluence of two elements, unique to Israel. The need of security, prosperity, and self-respect was as real in Israel as in other countries. But what was unique was that Israel's God was known as more than just a "divine" mandate for their nationhood. In their God they had discovered a freely-given love. Their God was therefore free, and had wider horizons than just Israel. The key element of transcendence had, for the first time, moved to the center of a People's experience.

Gradually, they became aware that their God must be the creator of all. But if God had created all, then all must share in his promises. Already, seven centuries before Jesus, this insight had fractured, if not broken, the common mold of national chauvinism. In grand Oriental images, the Israelites saw the other nations streaming to Jerusalem where God had shown himself most present. "Let us go to the hill of the Lord," the nations would sing, "so that he may teach us his ways . . . . Nations will hammer their swords into ploughs, never to go to war again." (Isaiah 2:2,4)

This would be part of the promised new world when there would again be 12 tribes, and Israel would be restored.

In the next century, a more profound insight into the promised future had come. Israel had ignored the prophet's warnings about their unfaithfulness to their God. The prophecies had proved true. Their capital city had been largely flattened. Most of God's People were now captive in a foreign land.[2]

Could they ever forget such a bitter and poignant experience?

The fertile fields and the vineyards destroyed,
briars growing on my people's land.
The palace is abandoned; the capital city deserted.
(Isaiah 32:13-14)

The brutal scenes of that invasion had burnt deep into their memories:

Swifter than eagles swooping down from the sky,
they
chased us down.
They tracked us down in the hills; they took us by
surprise in the desert.
(Lamentations 4:19)

National disaster and disgrace, and the prospect of a hopeless future. The natural sequel to all that was cynicism and despair.

Instead, Israel came to see that God had been right and they wrong. God had begged them, through the prophets, to "stop doing evil. See that justice is done—help those who are oppressed, give orphans their rights, and defend widows." (Isaiah 1:16-17) Such calls had been ignored. They saw this disaster as the result. "I stretch out my hands, and no one will help me . . . . But the Lord is just, for I have disobeyed him." (Lamentations 1:18)

Through decades of pain and desolation, this insight had come: their God was more than the protector of their nation; more than a person free to love; more than the creator of all, leading all to fulfillment. Deeper even than all this, *their God stood for wisdom and justice*. Even in the blood and dust of Middle Eastern power politics, he was guiding them to such a "world." The cost in pain had indeed been high; but the advance in insight was incalculable.

---

2. 587-537 B.C.E.

Between the Exile and Jesus

In the centuries between the return to their country in 537 B.C.E. and the life of Jesus, the conviction that God would restore Israel to full splendor took up and assimilated these developments. God's servant would "restore the tribes of Israel": he would restore the completeness and grandeur of when there had been 12 tribes. But in addition to that:

I will make you a light to the nations—
so that all the world may be saved.
(Isaiah 49:6)

Other insights, too, were gained in those intervening centuries. Helped by other civilizations, some had achieved a wider and more transcendent vision of God's promises.

But grasping such insights can never be automatic. Each individual and each group must take their own journey. Trivialization, or blindness, can always block our progress.

In Jesus' time, this dream of national wholeness was shared by all groups, but in impoverished ways. It had become elitist, or backward-looking, or just for political autonomy—depending on which group you belonged to. And the actual situation mirrored the limitations in vision. Israel lived as a nation of groups that despised each other. Only about two of the twelve tribes survived. Except perhaps for uniting for war against a common enemy, that promise of wholeness seemed impossible to achieve.

Jesus

That long-developing promise Jesus was claiming to take up. An ex-carpenter from Nazareth was saying: "What you have longed for is here." Even more remarkable, perhaps, was *the manner* of Jesus' claim.

Naturally anyone—mad or sane—could have made that assertion. But what people noticed in Jesus was not so much his asserting it but his living it. He didn't simply *say* "Israel is whole again": in all his relationships and his work he acted on that conviction. Nor did he simply follow any of the current or past expectations of how the dream would be realized. He invested it with a depth of humanity for which there was no precedent.

Why had he gone out of his way to offer friendship to toll-collectors, prostitutes and women? He had simply gone ahead and acted as if the barriers had been abolished and the nation was now whole.

They remembered the stories in which he had explained those relationships. Hadn't he, in one of them, used a number to denote wholeness? In his story of the Lost Sheep, the shepherd had done all he could to make the flock a whole hundred again. And when success had been achieved, what joy there had been! It was a joy, moreover, that had to be shared by *all!*

Equally, the prodigal son's father had longed for wholeness—for his family. He had killed the fatted calf, because *everyone* must join in the celebration.[3]

When Jesus declared the "cabinet" for the new regime, by appointing the Twelve, what did he believe would be the result?

It was obvious that he was not thinking of anything elitist or backward-looking. His actions showed that his only interest was in the profoundest needs of *every* type of person, and in their potentiality for the promised harvest.

Those people, for him, were much more than isolated individuals. They were "the lost sheep, the people of Israel." (Matthew 10:6) None of the other groups offered the hand of forgiving friendship to "the lost sheep". *They* existed for an elite; *Jesus* for the whole people.

What he presented to all the people was evidence that God had come to rule through him. The proof he offered was what they could see in himself, his relationships and his actions. "Do these not show," he was asking them, "that the tide of evil and estrangement has lost its grip on our condition? Isn't God fulfilling those promises and coming to the center of the human story?"

---

3. A fatted calf would have fed a whole village.

He was asking them to transform the self-centeredness so natural to us to a loving openness to human kinship. His meals, especially, could be for anyone a moving experience of that.

That was the thrust, *the general result*, of the new regime he was founding. With incalculable potential fruitfulness, Israel was being restored.

****

There is no clear evidence that Jesus knew *the specific shape* of the new regime and its policies.

How would the restored Israel be "a light to all peoples"? That he spoke to followers of that is probably shown by the swiftness with which they adopted that aim after his death. But Jesus himself showed no sign of having a *strategy* for that.

What kind of government would it have? Again, no clear-cut directives. The 12 were just a symbol—not a permanent institution.[4]

Among the increasing dangers of his last months, the Good News had somehow to be told to all Israel. Very likely, he and his followers believed that God would, somehow, bring about a breakthrough. Specific structures and strategies would emerge at that time.

What mattered for him was that the radically "new" had arrived. (Mark 2:21-22) The old religious barriers were down; imperfect values had been transcended; forgiveness was fully available; even the poor would be "happy"; God was inexpressibly close for all his restored people.

For the moment that was enough: the task of telling Israel. Obviously, that must soon involve a most dangerous decision. Galilee, where the opposition was more religious than political, would have to be exchanged for Israel's more daunting heartland. Jesus would have to take the three-day journey to Jerusalem itself.

---

4. So that his followers allowed it to disappear within 20 years after his death.

Seven

Decisions

Human destiny had changed; but no Jew could be a mere spectator. The case had been put, and the witnesses called: the jury were Jesus' own nation.

But couldn't you treat the evidence about God's "Kingdom" as just an intriguing possibility? Wasn't it just an interesting option, like what clothes you choose to wear?

It would have been so much more convenient to have regarded it so. Influential people in the town resented the Jesus movement; and, with the scarcity of jobs, it was unwise to alienate them. And what demands and even dangers might joining Jesus bring?

Other religious leaders facing such opposition might have issued tirades against such callowness. Jesus simply told stories. They weren't elaborate but situations you could easily feel involved in. Once you had gotten inside these situations, did you see a bolder reaction to be necessary? Here was a story about the excitement of a country-town wedding.

A Galilee Town Wedding

There was something regal, almost fairy-tale, about how such weddings were celebrated.[1]

The preparations were extensive: "A virgin is granted 12 months to provide for herself," an authority said. She prepared her clothes and adornments; the groom's side prepared the couple's home and the wedding feasts.

Jesus' story led up quickly to the most dramatic moment of all. The preparations are over; it is early evening; the bride is on her way. She's elaborately dressed and perfumed, riding in a carriage. It's not just a journey, but a triumphant progress through the town's main streets. There is singing, dancing, clapping; people play clarinets, gongs and bells. The town's gravest citizens would break off their business, and dance in the cavalcade. The bride is sitting in state, in her carriage, with a wreath as a crown: a youthful queen. On this tide of the town's enthusiasm, she being borne along towards the climax of the wedding ceremony: her entering the groom's home.

Now they had almost reached his house, the noise even greater than before. Darkness has fallen; torches light up the eager faces. The groom has been waiting at his house for the sounds of her arrival. Now he is coming out of the house to meet her, for the most solemn part of all. With some of her maids of honor, he will take her by the hand and lead her into the house that will be their home.

It is like watching a play on a large stage, when the climax has been reached. From either side of that large space, the protagonists move towards each other, though at this moment it is *not* the bride and groom but the maids of honor towards the groom. They must go and form the groom's cortege, so that he can immediately lead the bride in with solemn state. For this brief, penultimate moment, the spotlight is largely on the maids. And because night has fallen, and because etiquette so required, each maid must carry a lighted torch.

---

1. Here I give what is probably the original story. Matthew has altered some of the story, and its emphasis, for his purposes. (25:1-13)

Jesus' listeners anticipated no problem. Each maid was carrying a torch. Of course, it required regular replenishment; but a small jar of oil was normal equipment for torch-bearers. A few quick movements would suffice.

In minutes it will all be over: the groom "received," the bride led in. All eyes are following the climax of this well-known ritual with eagerness and delight. And then—but was it possible? Had insanity come to power? Five of the maids had brought no oil for this great occasion, so their torches had gone out.

Today, it would be like the U.S. President's cavalcade going from the White House to the Senate for a great speech, and finding on arrival that he had been left behind; or a coronation watched on TV by millions, and at the climax of the ceremony the discovery that the crown had not been brought.

Jesus' audience knew that this wasn't just a far-fetched story: they were being asked whether the cap fitted on them. Those maids' negligence was preposterous, but not of a trivial kind. It wasn't like letting your young child play with cans of paint in your best room. At the climax of a major story, the maids were in utter disarray. The groom would bring his bride into the house. The wedding ceremonies would go on. But the maids who had broken the thread of this celebration would creep home ashamed, and be a byword for years.

What was it like to be casual about God's coming through Jesus: not to respond with all your powers? It was like the negligence of those bridesmaids at that wedding: absurd at such a time.

The Other Side

The absurdity of negligence was the negative side of it. The opportunity was the other side. Again there was no beating of drums: no fervent or frenzied urging. Instead there is a bit of life you were asked to take hold of and judge. "Does it throw light on the decision before you?"

One story told of a poor day-laborer ploughing a field. The plowshare suddenly grates against a hidden jar. In those days before a banking system, when an enemy invasion threatened, you would probably bury your valuables in a jar and hope to recover them later if you survived.

The laborer had never seen such wealth as this hidden jar contained. Quickly he plunged it back into the earth, checking that no one else had seen him find it. He *must* buy that field: that was a treasure beyond his dreams.

For him to get the purchasing price would involve selling all he had. But he immediately grasped this opportunity of a lifetime, overjoyed at the unexpected chance.

It was the same in Jesus' story of a merchant in pearls who found a pearl of great value that he could buy at a low price. In the lives of both day-laborer and merchant, something marvelous had occurred. They were captivated by what they had found. They responded immediately, joyfully, with all their powers. "When you consider what you see in me," Jesus was asking, "should your response be like these?"

Eight

Confrontation

God's full Rule had not come. Support for Jesus had waned. Official opposition to him had stiffened.

Jesus told his friends he would go up to Jerusalem. He would go there for the Passover feast—as all male Jews must. They knew that Passover week, politically, was the most sensitive of the year. The feast celebrated God's promise to set his People free. Passionate longings would be alight in the great crowds.

From all the towns and villages of Galilee, people were going towards the capital. They were walking the three-day journey down one of the three routes. Often with wives and children, they were on pilgrimage to Jerusalem. Coming from every country were 100,000 Jews.

The journey of Jesus and his friends began pleasantly, down the west side of the lake. But by the end of the first day, they were going ever deeper into the Jordan valley, far below sea level. The mountains rose high above them on either side.

At least the journey gave them time to talk. Would this be the long-awaited showdown, when Jesus and they came to power? Was he going to confront the Jewish Establishment with the full force of his message? Jerusalem and its Temple stood for Israel as a whole. Would Jesus' message at last ring out from the center of the nation?

There was expectancy in Jesus' group, and in other groups they knew. Jesus clearly knew that the climax was close. But he didn't know its time or shape, or how it would take place.

A last night at Jericho brought back to Jesus memories of his time nearby with John. Then the tough ascent from 250 meters under sea level to the crest of Mount Olives, 760 meters above. That was the slowest—and one of the most dangerous—routes in all Palestine. But they had reached the last 20 miles of the year's most joyful pilgrimage. Anticipation of what they would see from the summit helped to give them strength. Perhaps they managed one of the pilgrimage songs along the winding, deserted road.

Jerusalem!

At the top came the sight they had longed for. Much of the panorama surrounding them was a sea of mountains. But there, opposite them, two miles across the Kedron valley, rode the Temple on its steep, cragged hill. The long east front towered grandly above them. The huge complex of shrine, square and administration dominated the city behind it.

They were awed by its splendor; proud of their national center. But to them, and to any Jew, the Temple was much more. It was God's "house" or "dwelling." It stood for God's effective presence with his People. Again their great pilgrimage songs rang out, in their lips or in their hearts:

> My heart breaks when I remember the past,
> when I went with the crowds to the house of God
> and led them as they walked along,
> a happy crowd, singing and shouting praise to God.
> (Psalm 42:4)

Now they went down past Bethany (where they would stay), along the tree-lined road, down to the river. Sheer above them now, glinting in the sunlight, were the huge grey-red walls of the east side of the Temple. Then up the steep hill, from the Kedron towards the city, jostling and laughing with the other pilgrims. There were shouts and impromptu dancing. People leapt and stamped with happiness. A feast was a time of joy—expressed as exuberantly as at any sport. In the melee Jesus may have made a gesture that he would indeed be king.[1] Then in through the city gate.

It was a moving experience, especially at Passover, to stand in the city walls. First might be your awareness of the great crowds all around you. A city that housed with difficulty 40,000 had, for this feast, three times that number.[2] God's People had assembled from all over the known world. They had taken hard, long journeys, from every land, to come to this city and its Temple.[3]

They loved these buildings as great monuments, things of beauty, their own nation's grand achievements. But above all, they loved them for what they embodied: the abiding presence, over so many centuries, of their God amongst their People.

They knew about its checkered history. They knew about the greed and lusts of God's representatives over the centuries. But in and through all this they believed God stood at their side, leading them towards a future beyond their dreams. *As a nation* they stood with God; as a nation they had come this week; and that nationhood came to great expression in these buildings they had now reached.

The Task

Jesus knew he had come to announce that this whole massive system must change. The promised future was now! God was taking *direct* power through him! The "whole" nation had

---

1. The Gospel account of the Triumphal Entry seems to contain more theological message than historical fact.

2. Because it was so high, the city was always short of water and of raw materials for industry.

3. "Countless crowds from countless cities came, some over land, others over sea, from east and west and north and south, at every feast." (Philo—a younger contemporary of Jesus)

assembled; that nation must now hear. They had come to celebrate what God had promised; this Galilean had it to give.

The huge buildings looked down on him, as he thought of the task he had. "A powerless Galilean upset us!" they seemed to say in their massive strength.

Over to the west, he could see Herod's palace that could house over a thousand men. To the north of the Temple, he could see the Fort Antonia barracks, manned by a whole cohort, always on the watch. And to the east was the Temple itself, with its squares and colonnades where more than 75,000 could stand. Together they represented the "reality" of contemporary Jewish life. Was Jesus of Nazareth proposing it was something he could change?

He knew that somewhere in the city was Pilate, with the power of Rome in his hands. He would have come up from his palace in Caesarea, to prevent major disturbances during the year's greatest feast.

How would Pilate react to talk of a new "king"? A younger contemporary of Jesus would echo Pilate's likely views: "Judea was full of robberies; and as the seditious groups found a person to head them, he was created a king immediately, in order to do mischief to the public."[4]

No one was under any illusions about how the Roman Procurator would react to sedition of any kind in his territory. It was 34 years since the Roman puppet, Archelaus, had suppressed a rebellion in this city at Passover time, killing 3,000 Jews. When Jewish indignation, soon after, had erupted into more violence in the city, the result had been 3,000 crucifixions.

The passions aroused by such butcheries had not gone away. Rome's dominance, and Pilate's career, depended on his showing toughness and taking shrewd preventative action. For a Procurator, the beginning of wisdom was the fear of revolt.

Few understood Pilate's situation better than the Jewish High Priest. Caiaphas would go down, even in Jewish history, as the archetypal opportunist. It was no accident that he held the office

---

4. Josephus

longer than any other High Priest. Appointed by Rome, he was Pilate's eyes and ears among his own people. Behind him stood his party, the Sadducees, despised but rich and powerful. They too believed it essential for their country to have a good relationship with their Roman overlord.

Public Challenge

So, ranged against Jesus lay these interlocking forces. On his side was his friends' enthusiasm—but did they really understand? There was also the urgent truth, and his authority to impart it. Could he convey that to his People before it was too late?

His tactics remained the same: stories that could illuminate but did not patronize. They could wake your conscience, so that you made your own judgement.

With mocking contempt, they were asking for his authority. But wasn't Israel, in Isaiah's words, a vineyard, tended and planted by God? Jesus reminded them of the many vineyards in Palestine leased out by absent landlords. What did such landlords do to their tenants who neglected their charge? Such tenants could find themselves dismissed, with others replacing them.

Then, like the rabbis, he drove his point home with two quotations: "The stone which the builders rejected turned out to be the most important." (Psalm 118:22) And "God will establish a kingdom that will never end." (Daniel 2:44-45—alluded to)

Them negligent tenants? *Jesus* the cornerstone? It was intolerable effrontery, but there was worse to come.

Jesus and his friends were in the Temple complex. People's eyes were upon him. Often garbled versions of his teaching were circulating in the city. Could he be the Messiah, or was he a crazy revolutionary?

Jesus had reached the Temple courtyard where you exchanged your currency to pay the Temple tax. It was a necessary transaction for essential Temple business.

Suddenly Jesus threw down one of the currency-changer's tables. It was a rejection, in miniature, of the present Jewish system. In an observant Jew like Jesus, it said "That system's time is over." In the very heartland of Israel, Jesus had announced a fuller world.

No arrest was made. Everyone knew the offence could not be tolerated. Caiaphas must be told.

Some left the Temple courtyard, towards the High Priest's palace.

Caiaphas

Caiaphas was accustomed to facing difficult situations. Several factors were involved in what this Jesus had done. But for Caiaphas they all pointed in the same direction.

Lightly, but very publicly, the whole Temple system had been questioned. The Sadducees, whom he led, derived their wealth from that system. Their opulent houses in the Upper City he had known and relished all his life. And wealth brought not just pleasure; it gave you the power to preserve Israel.[5]

Rapidly, he dismissed such thoughts. Jesus obviously had no power to subvert a system so established and widely popular.

It was the *political* dangers he could not brook. In the Jewish feast of Freedom, among the swirling, fervent crowds, a spark could easily lead to a disastrous conflagration. There would be much suffering by the people, and the good relationship with Rome would be lost.

It was urgent that he should accuse Jesus before Pilate. For the good of the people this foolish Galilean must die. It would be enough to mention Jesus' talk of a new kingdom. Everyone knew what Rome did to would-be kings.

---

5. Forty years later the Sadducees lost their wealth, their grand houses—and all their power.

Nine

Last Evening

What would happen now? The system had been publicly challenged. Would the response be swift and brutal? But could God's Messiah be snuffed out by human power? After that manifesto, mustn't triumph be imminent?

Everywhere there were crowds. The whole People seemed gathered. But not like a docile audience with no mind of its own. They wanted to be free, and they knew God brought freedom. Tonight, more than all others, this conviction blazed strongly. They would celebrate in their families their annual Freedom meal. They would evoke their experience of God's rescue and look eagerly towards the future. Through rite, meal and story they would recall their destiny to be God's People and free. This was the night when they expected the Messiah to come.

So, great hopes and great danger were the pressures of the hour. Was annihilation imminent, or would Jesus take command?

Jesus' answer to his friends was of the kind they had come to know. Partly it said, "no drama: life as usual. God will provide." That evening's business for all Jews was the annual Freedom meal. "Come to Jerusalem," he said, "this evening. It must also be ours."

The other part of his answer was to invest "the usual" with his own depth of meaning. What that was they would discover in the course of the meal.

A Room with a View

As Jesus' group assembled in the room they had hired in Jerusalem, there were obvious signs that this occasion was special.

The meal had to be held in Jerusalem—it was *the whole nation's* celebration. It was lavish and festive—even the poorest in Jerusalem had to be given four cups of wine.[1] It began later than the normal evening meal and you went to bed late—provision was made in the meal's customs for a nap after the dessert!

Each of the group had celebrated like this in Jerusalem year after year. They loved the sense the rite gave them that God's whole story on earth was theirs. From youngest child to oldest adult, a whole family would be drawn in. They were celebrating together the deepest certainties they had.

Great cries like this were threaded into the meal:

The Lord's love for us is strong
and his faithfulness is eternal.

In my distress I called to the Lord;
he answered and set me free.

The Lord is with me, I will not be afraid;
what can anyone do to me?
(Psalms 117:2; 118:5-6)

That, they believed, was the recurrent pattern of their past; they were confident it would reach its culmination in the future. Their nation was founded on the event of rescue from Egyptian slavery more than a thousand years ago; it was now fired by the conviction that a deeper freedom was in store.

---

1. If necessary, this was paid for from charity.

Jesus' group began, as did everyone, with wine and hors d'oeuvres served in an anteroom. The formality and stateliness added to the occasion. This evening Jesus had invited no women: only the Twelve. The Twelve were the core of the *restored* People. God's People was whole again, ready for its task. That added to the sense of being on the brink of a new world.

All Lost?

But the feeling of threat remained. Would they eat with him again? It was like holding a wedding round a death bed—doom in the midst of joy. A last meeting with a friend concentrates the mind and heart.

There come memories of the past: shared experiences that mean so much. You become more aware of how your friendship grew. With you, for the last time, is the person you love, who invests your life with meaning. From that you look out into the darkness of the future.

Jesus did not dismiss these feelings about him as sentimental or foolish. What he had done and had been for them were not just memories of the past. He was all these things still, and they had come to expression in this meal. His personality and his life were reaching their culmination.

Past Experience

When they had finished the hors d'oeuvres, they went in to dine. The solemnity and many details helped to highlight the topic, Freedom. But hadn't all the meals they had ever had with him been for that very purpose?

Memories flooded back of faces round his tables. People who had lived with social contempt and isolation had found welcome and respect there. Life for them at last was human and positive. They were finding themselves in a world where God was on your side. And not in isolated pockets of private relationships with God, but united as his People, sharing his work for the world.

The experience Jesus brought of God didn't happen in some obscure "soul." It happened in *all* of you coming towards full flower. First you had to see life as *for* you: it could come to great fruitfulness, whatever our inadequacies. Then you had to see your immediate relationships as the means of your fruitfulness: through our love and compassion we share in God's Rule. And lastly you had to be able to make some sense of what is beyond our immediate horizon: our country, other nations, life's vulnerability, and even death. It was in *these* things—at the heart of life—that Jesus showed God. In being a self, in your relationships, and in playing your part in the human story: it was in these central realities of all of us he experienced and showed them God. What this meant to themselves and to all those others was the point of all his meals.

The Echo of Memories

They reclined on their couches alongside the table, and the entire table top was brought in, already set for eating. The customs of a grand Roman dinner party in the most Jewish of feasts! Even the Jews could use, in their religion, cosmopolitan fashion!

As the Passover meal went on, there were questions and answers about aspects of the rite. "Why the bitter herbs?" "Why unleavened bread?" They made more poignant the experience of God's initial rescue. From the harshness of slavery, with no dignity and no hope, to their own country, self-respect, and human identity in the world.

This had been the thrust of their whole history. Tonight they revelled in that fact. "From darkness to light; from sadness to great joy."

But as the Twelve began these rites with Jesus, they knew tonight there was much more. As Jews they had always lived in the longing for fulfillment. *God* was their ruler: God, the Lord of all!

When fulfillment came, this would be cashed in full. The sludge of human history—injustice, war and waste—would be replaced by a humanity transformed to its true self.

How could you picture this achievement of human ripeness? In Jesus' time, and long before, it was pictured as a meal with God or his Messiah. Didn't the Jewish God love to satisfy our human desires? Didn't he provide and preside over human enjoyment? Wasn't he as intimate as any friend, to his "own dear People"?

And wasn't that dream now coming true? In all Jesus' meals, but particularly tonight, God seemed to be there in power, through his Messiah, "to remove the cloud of sorrow." There was a feeling of looking out to a world beyond all dreams. Inevitably, Isaiah's prophecy echoed in their ears:

> Here on Mount Zion (Jerusalem), the Lord Almighty will prepare a banquet for all the nations of the world. He will suddenly remove the cloud of sorrow that has been hanging over all the nations. The Sovereign Lord will destroy death forever! He will wipe away the tears from everyone's eyes.
> (Isaiah 25:6-8)

The Last Meal

These feelings were the context of the extraordinary meal that followed. Jesus began it in the way the man presiding did. He sat up on his couch and took a loaf of hard, tasteless bread. This was a central point in the evening: the formal start of the main meal.

As the presider, Jesus said on behalf of all a blessing over the bread. This was more than "just a prayer"; and it was more than just thanks. It was the group's sharing with God the point and scope of their lives. Unlike all other peoples, their God was at the heart of human history. "All you do is gift, is wisdom, brings women and men wholeness. This bread, this special meal, is your pledge of that fact." The presider used his own words, but this was their drift.

After that prayer, as was the custom, the Twelve[2] saw Jesus break the loaf into a piece for each person. He must now dis-

---

2. Though Judas had, by now, left him.

tribute to each member a piece of the bread. Into the silence that normally accompanied that, they heard him speak. *"You* take and eat," he said—for he himself wouldn't. "Take this bread that brings men and women wholeness, this share in the meal with God and his Messiah. Why? Because this represents my body[3], the person I am now. Haven't you come to know me as God's liberating power? Haven't you always seen me living for others in love? Eat this bread and enter into all that I am and do."

This was developed in the meal itself: the lamb, lettuce, fruit puree, bitter herbs, and more wine if you wanted. Through the questions and the answers and the sharing of many memories, they underlined and helped them revel in the significance of the evening. Then there were pauses, baffled faces, as they thought of tomorrow. The new world launched, but loss of Jesus, seemed an obscene contradiction.

That clash was made more poignant and even bitter through their experience of this meal. It wasn't just prayers, or great promises, or "religious ideas." It was the company of a friend whom they had gradually come to know.

It was so easy to engage his interest and concern. He held nothing of himself back, as he listened, spoke and prayed. He was completely theirs, both as individuals and as a group.

Round the table they would often catch his smile. You experienced in that look an empathy you could not describe. When you thought of it afterwards, it brought back memories of his stories: the reckless, warm compassion in the *Prodigal Son* story, or the practical and ready kindness of the Samaritan.

His laughter and simple joy recalled the village party of the shepherd when he had found his sheep. The sheer homeliness of Jesus made the similarity more complete. The Messiah was no grand warrior, to be followed from afar. He was one of them, round this table, more human than they had ever known.

---

3. The word didn't mean just physical body, but the whole person in his/her significance and effectiveness.

"New Covenant"

At the end of the main meal, as the presider, Jesus said a prayer of wonder and thanks (a "Eucharist") over the third cup of wine. In behalf of all, the prayer celebrated all God was doing for humankind.

Contrary to the custom of each drinking from his own cup, Jesus now asked them to share in the same cup. Those present knew the current expectation that when God came fully to his people they would all share from the same cup, reconciled to each other and to God. As they were drinking from the cup—usually in silence—Jesus expressed the meaning this had for him. "This cup," he said, "is the new covenant in my blood."

So he *would* die. He had confirmed that they would lose him, that the obscenity would happen. But through his death would come fulfillment, described long ago as "a new covenant."

They struggled to make sense of that intolerable contradiction. It might be a long time before much light would come.

Yes, they knew about covenants, as Orientals and as Jews.

As *Orientals,* they knew they could be instruments that changed your whole world. A great lord would pledge ("covenant") himself to help and protect the weak and powerless. They would no longer be hopelessly enslaved to misery, but in charge of their own lives.

As *Jews,* the Twelve knew such covenants as the cornerstones of their whole history. All their hopes—their very identity—rested on those promises. Through God's making a covenant with them they had become a People, with a land and a future. God's covenants with them had made love and faithfulness the surest things in a world rife with greed and ruthless power.

When Jesus said "covenant," all this came before them: a whole history given meaning and concrete shape by a loving, faithful God:

> showing his constant love to a thousand generations,
> loving you and blessing you, so that you will have
> many children.

No people in the world will be as richly blessed as
you.
(Deuteronomy 7:9, 13-14)

As God had made further covenant pledges—always built on
the first—there had always been that thrust towards unimagin-
able fulfillment. One day, a prophet said, a "new covenant"
would achieve this. (Jeremiah 31:31) By announcing a "new
covenant," Jesus was saying that day is here.

That didn't surprise his friends. God was coming to rule in
Jesus. But Jesus was saying "this will happen in my blood."

Death

He wasn't talking directly about the red fluid in our veins. By
"blood" an Oriental meant life: you as alive, with your personal
powers. But since blood flows away, it often suggested losing
your life. It was through Jesus' losing his life that the new
covenant would come.

Jesus would sacrifice all he was—his love of life, his powers,
his self—so that the time of harvest could come for all.

But this wouldn't just happen "from outside" them. Jesus had
never treated anyone as a sponge simply to *receive* God's gifts.
By drinking from this cup they would commit themselves to his
whole stance to life and to all that would flow from that. As his
"Twelve"—his core community—they would do that for everyone.

The shock and the growing sadness made it hard for them to
understand. Yes, loving service was his way—God's Rule coming
through compassion, not selfish power. But had that to lead to
his death?

Of course they had seen the mounting risks. But the confron-
tations of this week had brought them exhilaration, not fear.
They *had* to be proof of Jesus' confidence that God was about to
give him open power.

Now

Is it possible to express in modern language what Jesus intended by this meal?

We have to start from the obvious fact that it was for religious people. "The religious person is one who grasps his or her life within a larger historical and cosmic setting. He/she sees him/herself as part of a greater whole, a longer story in which he/she plays a part. Song, ritual and vision link that person to this story. They give that person a past and a future."[4]

Every Jewish meal was that; and so especially was that of Passover. Through song, ritual and vision you strengthened your link to God's story.

Jesus' claim was that that story now centered on him. Through him, God was available to a degree that he had never been before. You could see more clearly what God is like. You could be enriched by God's power. All of this was available by joining Jesus and living in his way.

The purpose behind this wasn't different from what had gone before Jesus—it was simply moving into a fuller key. God, for a Jew, had always been the person who wanted to share his fullness with everyone.

What Jesus was trying to do towards that becomes clearer if we recall our experience of ourselves. We know that our personality is composed of three interconnected elements: my self, my personal relationships, and my wider relationships and horizons. To the extent that any of these are stunted in me, so am I as a person. To the extent that they are balanced and well-developed, so am I a fuller human being.

But in Jesus' time and ours, to achieve that is not easy. It's easier to duck our responsibilities or not to bother with other people. It's easier to stick to my little set, and forget my kinship with others and the wider story. "I don't care about the threat to the ozone layer: I'll be dead when disaster comes."

---

4. Harvey Cox, *The Feast of Fools*, Cambridge Mass., 1969, p. 14.

What makes it particularly difficult to be really human is a thing we call "the system." "My group does things this way. Perhaps it's unjust; but why should I buck the system?" There can be a hardness and irresponsibility in such inhuman stances that one rarely finds in individuals.[5]

All these kinds of attitudes that wreck our humanity were met by Jesus as well as by ourselves. He met them in the people who opposed him, and even in his friends.

In himself and in his teaching, what kind of person did he show himself to be? Was there a great strength of purpose, combined with gentleness and flexibility? Were his relationships warm, open, and sensitive, fired by a longing for people's good? And so far as wider horizons were concerned, did all this rest on a vision of all our destinies?

Our measuring of *any* man or woman depends on our answers to such questions. If we say that God made available a fuller humanity in Jesus, that must be based on those criteria.

But if Jesus was to be, in Genesis' words (1:26), the "human projection" of God, wouldn't God have to be manifested in him also in his dying? In fact, in Jesus' dying the deepest thrusts of his life found expression: his love and trust in God, and his loving commitment to people.

That was one sense in which Jesus died "for all." He was for us *a model of God in human people.*

The other sense in which he died "for all" was linked with his *founding God's restored People.* The presence of just the Twelve and much else showed that this was what this meal was about.

Membership in it would be the chief means offered to all to become like Jesus and to share in his abiding life and work: a work characterized by ready self-sacrifice, putting the other first.

---

5. My interpretation of Jesus' death owes much to John Macquarrie, *Principles of Christian Theology*, London 1977. This sentence is virtually a quotation from page 262.

Ten

Trial and Death

Caiaphas, the arch-survivor, went quickly to action. Immediately he summoned his senior colleagues to decide the charge to be made against Jesus. He ordered the Temple soldiers to find the man among the huge crowds. Judas, one of the Twelve, had offered to lead them to him.[1]

Even without Judas' help, the task of finding Jesus, at evening, might not have been too difficult. Most of the pilgrims had to sleep outside the city, under canvas, amongst their townsfolk. Information about Jesus' plans might quite easily have been sought.

From the supper Jesus had gone, with his companions, to the Gethsemane garden. He knew death was at hand. He faced the horror of dying and the utter failure of all his work. All that would remain of those great hopes and promises would be a carcass on a cross.

Of course he had known the dangers of coming to the city with his claim at this feast. The enormity of his Temple

---

1. Probably the lack of any tangible "victory" had made him lose hope that Jesus was, in fact, the Messiah.

demonstration was obvious, and calculated. But for his complete faith in God, the whole thing was absurd.

Before the Temple soldiers found him, he had been engulfed in great waves of despair. God had let him down, forsaken him; yet the Kingdom *would* come. "Your will be done, your Rule come," he had cried, from that despair. His *experience* of those years of healing, hope and fellowship could not be effaced. He *knew* the Rule of God. Despair would not get the mastery.

The arrest was made as offensively as the troop knew how: but as a radical critic of the Temple, Jesus had expected that. More poignant was the utter dismay in his companions' faces.

Now through the garden towards the city. For the last time the steep ascent from the Kedron valley and in through the city gates. No escort now from the jubilant expectant followers of a few days before. The Temple soldiers were lugging him impatiently towards Caiaphas' palace.

What would happen now? Caiaphas' likely reaction would have been obvious to any Jew. For 12 years he had been high priest—the leading Jewish official. At any time he could have been fired at will by the Roman Procurator (of the 18 high priests in 60 years, only three ruled for more than two years[2]). Caiaphas had lasted so long only through his being Rome's most trusted eyes and ears.

He presided over and embodied the Jerusalem Establishment. Like the city itself, this Establishment was wealthy and proud. But a city with only one source of income is obviously vulnerable. For all classes in Jerusalem, that one source was the Temple.[3] Jesus' declaration that it would be replaced was like publicly questioning the war effort of your country when the enemy is at the door. Immense feelings of anger were bound to be unleashed.

Had the questioning come from a lone crank, a flogging might have sufficed. But here was someone with a following, who talked of a new king. Didn't he come from Galilee—the seedbed

---

2. From 6 C.E.-66 C.E.

3. There was no industry in Jerusalem; and the surroundings were not very fertile.

of the revolutionary movement? Hadn't he promised "equality" to the poor—90° of the population? Hadn't he been linked with John the Baptist, who had been "eliminated" by Herod for his politically dangerous "eloquence"?[4]

Caiaphas' palace had been reached. Jesus was brought in for questioning. Had he, or had he not, dared to threaten the Temple system?

"Yes, God will replace the Temple"—his own role was not his point.[5] Caiaphas and his colleagues had no doubt what must now follow. The system from which their wealth and power came must be protected against this man. Potential rebellion must be thwarted, lest they be dismissed by Rome from power. The man must be sent to Pilate on a charge that would certainly bring a death sentence. "Threatening the Temple" might not suffice—even at Passover time. To make death entirely certain, Jesus was charged with claiming to be king.

Pilate

A Jew arrested on a charge of treason knew what kind of reception to expect in Pilate's palace. His soldiers came from cities of a Greek culture, and fanatically hated Jews. In their coarse and brutal ways, they would give vent to their contemptuous hatred.

The rough treatment from the soldiers was but a prelude. Caiaphas wanted Jesus to be dispatched quickly. To give breathing space for public protest was unthinkable. So the trial before Pilate was quickly begun.

Was Pilate as evil as Jews of that time described him? Two who never became Christians spoke of his "ceaseless and intolerable cruelty."[6]

---

4. Josephus

5. The Gospel accounts were written in the light of later insights into Jesus' role and status. It is *possible* that he claimed to be Messiah at the trial, but not "Son of God" in the later sense—the phrase would not then, in Jerusalem, have borne that meaning.

6. Josephus and Philo.

Brutal he was, and obstinate—but perhaps more as a victim than a master of his circumstances. He was far below the senatorial grandees. As such, he had been given one of the less desirable postings.[7] Without the political clout of a senator or the large estates to fall back on, his career and even his life were more vulnerable to the changes in the emperor's favor.

Success—and even survival—depended on his skillful juggling of three "balls." He had to satisfy the emperor, far away in Rome; he had to satisfy the Roman legate in Syria—his immediate supervisor; and he had somehow to win and keep the favor of the Jewish Establishment, especially the high priest. Each of these could complain and win his removal and disgrace.[8]

In these circumstances, could he reject the wishes of such a "reliable" high priest as Caiaphas? True, there were no clear signs of Jesus being an actual threat to the country's peace. He had some following, but no army; he hadn't pillaged or killed. Had there been any signs of such things, Pilate wouldn't have needed a "tip off" from Caiaphas, and not only Jesus but also his followers would have been quenched with ruthless power.

But Jesus—Caiaphas claimed—wanted to be some kind of "king." Not to order the fellow's death would be an affront to the Jewish Establishment and could seem to admit a rival king to the Emperor. The matter needed no serious thought from Pilate. Almost perfunctorily he murmured the formal sentence that he had so often pronounced before: "You will go to the cross."[9] The feelings of the convicted man before him were hardly his concern. The glint of anticipation in the soldiers' eyes caused him no surprise.

---

7. Bracketed with other postings on the least civilized fringes of the Roman Empire by the near-contemporary Roman historian Tacitus. He wrote of the inhabitants as "half- barbarian."

8. Six years later, Pilate was removed from his post because of a complaint to the legate about his cruelty.

9. It has been estimated that there were 6,000 executions in his years as Procurator.

"Unnecessary"

So, one of the most horrible deaths, and yet quite "unnecessary." Like a road accident that kills a child or a young couple, it shouted the question: Why?

If Jesus had not come up to Jerusalem and made the Temple protest, he would not be a condemned man now, facing this death. Neither Caiaphus nor Pilate would have had an urgent reason for proceeding against him. His talk of "king" and of equality might eventually have led to trouble. But Jesus had so far gained less public prominence than his former leader, John the Baptist. There were much greater political dangers for the country's leaders to contend with. Jesus could probably have counted on several more years of life and work if he had kept to Galilee.

So why had he come? The demonstration in the Temple showed its utter deliberateness. Whether God "intervened" or not, Jesus had decided to risk death now, and one of the most dreadful. If we are to understand his story, we must try to find the explanation for this fact.

Freely engaging in a horrible war, or rescuing a child from a blazing house: engaging in such actions normally arises from one of our central convictions. Jesus was convinced that marvelously, through him, a new birth was taking place. In that complex thing we call the world, he had discovered that to be so.

He had experienced that in the healing of those squalid beggars; in the toll-collectors coming home; in men and women being rescued from self-centeredness; in people's putting kindness first.

Yes, such things were known before: in every time and in every place. Women and men had achieved the humanity which by nature was theirs. What Jesus had discovered was that this humanness would win and was moving now towards its climax.

It was the scale and scope of this development that brought the joy and the commitment to sharing it. It wasn't "knockdown" or abstract. Neither toll-collectors nor prostitutes were an "ideal" set of people! Poverty and great frustration made life a tough struggle.

It was in *this* that Jesus had found his movement. It wasn't in abstraction or mere principle. It mirrored a personal reality: a person of kindness and healing, of calling home and service. For the movement towards full humanity was the radiance of God.

Every person was called to be lit by that radiance, for every person could direct his or her life towards love and healing. In that way, they would be in touch with their true selves, with other people, and with their future.

This was the Rule of God—God was at the center of this movement. "Your kingdom come. Your will be done." Back in Galilee, Jesus could have enjoyed again its people and the rest, but not as part of the movement towards humanity's full brightness. He had to call the whole nation to that. Death, and even a death like this, had to be risked.

Execution

Everyone knew what kind of death that was. Its purpose was to subdue the toughest and most unruly by terrifying even them. It was used only on slaves and subject nations, never on Roman citizens. One Roman commentator called it "the worst extreme of torture";[10] another Roman showed vivid awareness of its horror.[11]

Jesus was taken down from Pilate's Hall to begin the ordeal. It always began with an extreme flogging. Blood flowed in streams. The wounds, the pain, and the weakening through loss of blood were all part of the official strategy. All helped to make the public spectacle that followed an even grimmer warning to potential rebels.

Now the public parade through the streets to the place of execution northwest of the city walls. The beam of the cross was carried—the upright stake was already in place. Jesus was already too weak to carry the beam, because of the loss of blood.

---

10. Cicero

11. "Weighed down on one's own wound, already deformed, swelling with ugly weals on shoulders and chest, and drawing the breath of life amid long-drawn-out agony." (Seneca)

This kind of punishment was intended to cause the utmost indignity. The body was stripped naked before the nailing. The soldiers could give full rein to their contempt and hatred.

The heel bones and the forearms were nailed to the gnarled olive wood. To prolong the duration of the agony, the man "sat" on a piece of wood. As well as the tearing of the nerves and flesh, there was the heaving of the body in the desperate fight for breath.

Minutes seemed like hours. Death could still be a long way off. Groups of onlookers mocked his ridiculous claims: "This naked criminal a king!"

Some of his women followers stood by him still. All the men had fled. He had called the whole nation to its peace. What was left of all those hopes?

It was unnecessary, sterile, brutish. Where *could* you find God in this?

Eleven

Resurrection

The chief question about Jesus is: What *really* happened next?

You had had that life, and that shambles of a death. Humanity would be enriched by the quality of that life. The man's followers would base a religion on it, with a variety of results. But, with his last gasp on that cross, was Jesus' life ended?

"Of course it was," many will reply. "Death is the end for all." Jesus' first followers soon came to believe that he still lived. "If Christ has not been raised, then your faith is a delusion" (1 Corinthians 15:17). An immense claim, obviously. But was it a fraud or an illusion?

The closer we get to what it meant, the more we shall see that, if it were fact, it would be the answer to all our noblest dreams. Unfortunately, that cannot alone prove that we can trust the claim. With so much at stake, we are obliged to make an objective assessment. We must use Bible scholarship to try to discover what Jesus' followers really experienced.

*   *   *

In Jesus' last hours, he had endured more than great pain. Except for a few women, he had died abandoned by all his friends. His male followers had fled, their great hopes in ruins.

They had hoped and believed that God would publicly intervene. Through some marvelous act of power, Jesus would be declared God's Messiah. But no intervention had come. Jesus was crucified and had died.

One who died on a cross was "accursed of God." (Deuteronomy 21:23) The man on whom they had placed their hopes was not just deserted, but disgraced. Most of them fled to Galilee and resumed their earlier lives. Nothing seemed more dead than the whole Jesus movement.

Then, in quite a short time, there came a total change. Instead of taking refuge in Galilee, they risked the same fate as Jesus and went to Jerusalem. There they claimed the disgraced "rabble-rouser" had risen from the dead. No longer frightened and crushed, they acted with huge conviction.

Their new-found courage did not evaporate when dangers came. They were ready to make great sacrifices, even their own lives. Yet they never had the look of mere visionaries or fanatics.

So, in a group of apparently balanced people we see a change that was massive, profound and resistant to great pressure. That, at least, is a certain fact, which we must try to account for.

At this point in the enquiry, it's easy to take a false step. We can take it for granted that we should start with the Gospel stories about Jesus being seen. But the earliest Gospel, Mark's, was written at least 35 years after he had died, while there is a whole block of evidence that takes us back to the early 30s.

The Gospel stories at first sight suggest that Jesus was simply restored to the human life we know: a fishing trip, some meals, and fairly ordinary conversation. It seems a touching, but temporary, restoration of a friendship. But the *earlier evidence* opens up a very different perspective. So do the Gospel accounts, we shall see, when we turn to what they are really saying.

Our first question must be: What did the witnesses believe had happened? Then we must assess on what they based their belief.

What Did the Witnesses Believe Had Happened?

The Earlier Evidence

We could start with a public letter Paul wrote to the Corinthians in 54 C.E. There he reminds them of "the Good News, which I preached to you, on which your faith stands." He reminds them also that it wasn't just *his* Good News or "gospel": it was an heirloom that had been passed from one Christian to another over the 24 years since Jesus' death. Like the others, he had received it in solemn trust, kept it intact, and duly passed it on.[1] It was that "Christ was raised to life" and had "appeared" to Peter, the Twelve and others.

Paul himself would have been taught this in Damascus in 32 C.E. and would have talked about it when he had visited Peter in Jerusalem a few years later. (Galatians 1:18) So Paul's evidence takes us to within a few years of Jesus' death. He would have lost all credibility if he had claimed this to be the central Christian conviction, if that hadn't been the case.[2]

Part of the evidence he submits is the "appearance" to Paul himself. On his way to Damascus, he had had an experience that radically changed his whole life. Before it happened, Paul had hated this new "heresy" as a cancer in Judaism. These people followed an "accursed" man: they must be scoured from the earth. On his way to destroy this disgraceful teaching in that city, he believed he had "seen" Jesus. For him, what happened then proved Jesus right, and the fierce persecutor became a Christian.

As with the other witnesses, this was much more than just proof of a belief. In all the tumultuous years ahead, fighting against great odds, what drove him on and made him joyful was

---

1. The phrases he uses here had that meaning, both for possessions and for teaching.

2. As a great biblical scholar wrote: "No statement could be more emphatic or unambiguous. Paul is exposing himself to the criticism of resolute opponents, who would have been ready to point to any flaw in his credentials or in his presentation of the common tradition" (C.H. Dodd, *Studies in the Gospels* [ed. Nineham] Oxford 1957, p. 28).

his conviction that Jesus was risen. "All I want is to know Christ and to experience the power of his resurrection." (Philippians 3:10) Jesus' resurrection was now the great transforming power at the center of his life—not a bizarre last chapter of someone else's life.

There is other evidence that takes us back to the first years of Christianity. It consists of statements of what was held to be the core of Christian belief. These earliest creeds are the best means of beginning to see what these people believed had happened.

The First Statement

At first sight, these earliest creeds can seem disappointing. They simply say that "God raised Jesus from the dead." They don't tell us what Jesus looked like or what he did and said. It's like telling a friend, "I've just gotten married," without describing your spouse or your wedding day. But if you know both partners well, and have long hoped for them to marry, then the announcement won't be dull but will bring you great joy.

In fact, the whole of Jesus' public life had been about the question of whether there was really a "marriage" between two things. One of them was everything that Jesus did and stood for. With massive authority, he had claimed that God's full power was present through him. But that could be of no lasting good unless it was "married" to God's validation. In fact, Jesus' claims were mocked and hated, and eventually brought his death. Where was the God he had strongly claimed was behind him? Where was the "marriage" that was announced by "God raised Jesus from the dead?"

"Jesus"

"Jesus," in that statement, was all we have glimpsed in this book. It meant more than a human being with specific physical and other characteristics. It meant more than their friend whom they had lived and worked with and greatly loved. "Jesus" here meant the person who had made those great claims and the new world he had publicly promised. Emotionally, and physically, they had staked everything on that. They had faced resentment, even hatred, from their own people. What had kept them going was their conviction that, through Jesus, the God of love was close to the "harvest."

Then, with Jesus' death, this whole edifice had collapsed like a pack of cards. The man who had made those claims in the name of God had become a helpless, degraded spectacle, and "accused of God." They had lost a friend, and their role—how could they continue to make Jesus' claims? Their bitterest loss was that the world Jesus had promised as imminent had proved to be a chimera.

Where was it all now: the good news for the poor, freedom for the oppressed, real hope of overcoming the inhumanity and degradation that glared at you in every town? Where was the discovery of an intimate God, joyfully by your side? Where was the sense of standing on the threshold of great hopes like these? With Jesus' death, all that had gone forever.

Then quickly, and together, they changed from despair to total confidence. They had an experience that convinced them that all they had known in Jesus was now authenticated by God. They were experiencing it transforming themselves and others. They now knew at first hand that God's kindness *did* rule, that a great future *was* secure. Humanity, and all creation, had entered a different sphere.

Experiences like that cannot be described as you would a washing machine or a chair. It wasn't like a car or a street or an ordinary conversation. It was like our experience of deep friendship, of sublime joy or of a beauty that entrances us. We can't describe them, but only suggest them, using the power of symbols.

The earliest Christian statement of belief, therefore, "God raised Jesus from the dead," was a means of conveying not mere shape but *deep meaning through a symbol*. It was not intended to convey the kind of meeting you could photograph.[3] The statement was a symbol that drew its significance from people's profoundest experiences. It was chosen as the best way available of expressing what they were now convinced had happened.

---

3. When Paul encountered the risen Jesus, those with him saw nothing. They weren't open to what was being shown.

Other symbols were also used. In these earliest years after Jesus' death, they were struggling to express what this meeting with the risen Jesus involved. Later, we can look at what the other symbols said.

"Resurrection"

The resurrection symbol had to do with something we experience in all our important actions. In all of them, we need to have some confidence that the outcome of our actions will correspond to what we've done. The farmer must have confidence that sowing seed will normally lead to harvest; the employee that a day's work will normally lead to a fair wage. In our human relationships, also, we need a certain pattern in a relationship and a confidence that it will endure.

The key belief of the Jews was that you could trust that life had a pattern and was moving in a certain direction. They believed that this derived from the character of God. God's "personality" was stamped on everything that existed. God had been revealed to them as always true to himself as the loving and faithful one. That integrity of God to himself was the main force in human life, so far as human beings allowed it to be. "The mountains may depart, the hills be shaken, but my tender kindness will never be shaken." (Isaiah 54:10)

Because their God was like that, so, basically, was all authentic human life. Yes, there were great disasters; and you could choose to be fickle and unloving. But, at the end of the day, it would be such a God who would win. The key to a fruitful life was to share in and rely on God's total integrity. If you lived loyal to this God, you could count on fruitfulness.

This belief was obviously crucial to the great questions we all have to ask: What kind of person should I become? What kind of future can I look forward to? Can I somehow fail to have a successful life? Central to the answers was God's total trustworthiness—not just when the mood took him, as with other gods, but because of this integrity.

It wasn't only the great questions about our destiny that this conviction affected. "There is absolutely no concept in the Old

Testament with so central a significance for all the relationships of human life as God's 'integrity'."[4]

It is moving to find examples of this conviction at least eight centuries before Jesus' time:

> The Lord is a refuge for the oppressed,
> a place of safety in times of trouble.
> Those who know you, Lord, will trust you;
> you do not abandon anyone who comes to you.
> (Psalm 9:9)

It wasn't a private deal with the religious: a solace for the few. It was the basic pattern of all creation: an assurance that made the whole earth shout for joy:

> The Lord is king! Earth, be glad!
> Rejoice, you islands of the sea!
> The Lord rules with integrity and justice.
> He gives you the early rain in his integrity,
> he makes the rain come down
> and the threshing floors are full,
> the vats overflow with wine and oil.
> (Psalm 97:1-2 and Joel 2:23ff)

Sometimes, we find broad canvas-strokes like those: songs of all creation. More often, the focus is on our human actions.

Those who respond to the opportunity of reflecting God's integrity in their lives act in a way that mirrors that quality. Such a person "takes care of his/her animals, gives generously to others, and knows the rights of the poor. He or she deals with disputes fairly—even with foreigners. He or she takes a human relationship seriously."[5] All of these you had to work at: integrity couldn't be had on the cheap.

The fruit would be a sound, healthy life, because it was consonant with God's character and direction. It brought an intimacy with God: a loving, stable relationship. (Hosea 2:20-25) And the reward of this integrity would be "to see your (God's) face, and to gaze my fill on your likeness." (Psalm 17:15)

---

4. Gerhard von Rad, *Old Testament Theology*, Vol. 1, Edinburgh, 1962, p. 370.

5. Proverbs 12:10; 21:26; 29:7 and I Samuel 24:17.

That this integrity of God would win in our world was utterly dependable:

> The heavens will disappear like smoke;
> the earth will wear out like old clothes.
> But the deliverance I bring will last for ever;
> the victory of my integrity will be final.
> (Isaiah 51:6)

The joy brought by this assurance rings out often in the Bible. It was like a bird protected by its mother; like enjoying a great feast; like slaking your thirst from a river. It was like light in the darkness or like grass sparkling after the rain.[6]

Because of its intimacy and stability, it would endure in spite of great misfortune. God was "a place of safety in times of trouble and abandoned no one who came to him."

In those insecure, changing times, this trust brought great peace. But the Jewish religion was not a set of beliefs set in stone, never to be changed. The beliefs grew from people bringing together their present experience with the insights of Scripture. That involved taking a hard look at what was happening in your life. Two centuries before Jesus' death, that kind of realism raised tough questions about that trust in God.

Twelve Years of Terror (175-163 B.C.E.)

If God was really a ruler of integrity, he would reward the good and punish the bad. But in the terrible years from 175 B.C.E., this was flagrantly not the case. In earlier periods, great suffering had been interpreted as God punishing his people for their unfaithfulness. God would correct them for a time, for their own eventual good. But the suffering and butchery of this decade could not be accounted for in this way, because the chief victims of the persecution were people heroically loyal to God.

The persecutor was their own king, Antiochus IV. Soon after his accession in 175, he began undermining the religion of faithful Jews.

---

6. Psalm 36:7-8; and 2 Samuel 23:3

It began with his replacing the high priest, so as to pocket a bribe. This soon led to deeply offensive customs being imported from abroad—even naked athletic contests, close to the Temple.

Fired by disgust at what they saw as a blatantly immoral rule, the citizens of Jerusalem drove the king's officials from the city. They were taking advantage of the king's fighting a war in Egypt. But their success in this was shortlived.

Antiochus returned to Palestine in 169. "As furious as a wild animal, he ordered his men to murder everyone—men and women, boys and girls; even babies were butchered." (2 Maccabees 5:11-13)

The next year Antiochus was again fighting in Egypt. His campaign ended in humiliation. "He turned back to his kingdom in a rage and tried to destroy the religion of God's People" (Daniel 11:29-30). He took every possible step to desecrate and abolish the Jewish religion. Even observing the Sabbath privately was punishable by death.

For the majority of Jews, the 12 years of this reign were often a living hell. Though previous tyrants were seen as beasts, Antiochus was believed to be the worst. It wasn't just the killings and the burnings, the desecration and corruption. Worse was the realization that disloyalty to God brought great rewards, while loyalty brought disaster. Was their God really "a place of safety in times of trouble"? Did he really "abandon no one who came to him"? Had their central conviction of God's integrity simply broken in their hands?

It was in this crucible that a belief in resurrection found a certain shape. There was the experience of horror and hopelessness: there was no question of disguising that. Jewish faith was never a matter of evading reality.

They held that reality, squarely faced, up to the light of the Scriptures. God was trustworthy, loyal and loving and would vindicate good people: they knew that was part of Scripture's message. But in one of their Bible's greatest hymns to God's integrity, wasn't there another important dimension as well?

God was praised there as the "everlasting rock," a refuge for the needy, the God you could always trust. But he was also the sovereign Lord "who will destroy death for ever." (Isaiah 26:4; 25:4; 25:8) God's crowning work would be to remove the curse of death.[7]

Though they had possessed this prophecy for about 200 years, and others like it much longer, it took this searing crisis to bring that insight to flower. This life isn't all there is. God's plan extends beyond these fleeting years. The horizons of human hope had immeasurably extended.

In the 170 years still to pass before Jesus, this belief in wider horizons to human life took many forms. The picture was sometimes of resurrection of the body; sometimes only of the spirit. Resurrection could be only for Israel or the "holy"; or it could be for everyone. All that was certain was that it would be for the purpose of vindicating God's being true to his essential character of bringing goodness and giving life, and God's own vindication of good people. His love and faithfulness *would* prove to be the deepest and ultimate force in all that exists.

"God Has Raised Jesus from the Dead"

In Jesus' time, every Jew praised God every day as the one who "curbed the proud, judged the ruthless, sent down dew on the earth." God was the one who would make our way of life fully human, and overcome the gross inhumanity. It was in that context that they also celebrated him as the one who "raises from the dead."[8]

So resurrection would not be a thin kind of "survival." It would be the culmination of God's work for the human family he loved. It would be his bringing humanity to its full growth and flowering, and his vindication of those who had worked to that purpose.

All this is the key to understanding what the Christians meant when they said that *the* Good News was that "God raised Jesus from the dead." Some people "saw" the risen Jesus—what

---

7. Genesis 3:19 "records" that curse.

8. Both quotations in this paragraph are from a prayer that all Jews, in Jesus' time, were expected to say three times daily.

"saw" meant we must ask at a later point in our enquiry. It wasn't an ordinary meeting you might have photographed—not all those present saw it (e.g., Acts 9:7). No witnesses attempted to describe Jesus' face or gestures.

Though they couldn't describe physical features, they had to try to express the encounter's meaning. The word they chose was "resurrection": "God has *raised* Jesus from the dead."

To their Jewish contemporaries, we have seen, the basic meaning of that was clear. Would you see a physical body like ours or something different? On that, views diverged. The exact contours of a fuller world were not surprisingly elusive.

What was clear was that such a claim essentially consisted of two things. One was *about God*. Their daily prayer had come true! God's work for the human family was now coming to flower. So it was a claim to an encounter with the transforming, creative power of God.

That power was God at his most typical: the full expression of his characteristics and his plan for the world. Behind it, if you like, was the full "weight" of his personality—the love and faithfulness.

These witnesses were claiming to have had evidence, in Jesus, that this was now happening. A person who had such evidence would obviously have feelings of joy and security. They would feel embraced by, and inseparable from, the gracious kindness in their midst. This "resurrection" experience was, in fact, most prominent, as we shall see in the earliest Christian evidence.

This presence of God in human life was only one implication of the "resurrection" claims. The other was what it said *about Jesus*. We have seen that "resurrection" was partly about how God would vindicate, not just his nature, but also those who stood for truth and goodness. To claim that "resurrection" has happened in an individual implied vindication for all he or she had stood for. In spite of that shameful death, therefore, the message of Jesus was true. God *was* coming to rule through Jesus. And *the kind of God coming was the one reflected in Jesus' actions and stories*. This other strand of the "resurrection" claim also lies deep in the earliest evidence.

So far, we have taken what "resurrection" meant to Jesus' contemporaries and recalled very briefly how it corresponded with what we find in the lives of Christians. But what kind of "appearance" could have evoked such a massive claim?

Our question already points to the difficulty we face. If all that had been claimed was that Jesus, after his death, still lived in the way we do, then the kind of "appearance" that showed that would be like our own meetings with our friends. But what *this* "appearance" showed the witnesses was that a "new creation"[9] had begun: that the fullest dimensions of God's power had entered into our situation.

Grappling with this question, therefore, is much more difficult than we might have thought; and it is wiser to postpone it until all the evidence is in.

Most of the rest of the evidence is how this power came to effect in a wide range of Christian people. "The resurrection" was not just a claim provoked by some "appearances" to a few. It was also the hallmark, the thrust, of any genuine Christian life.

In parts of the New Testament, we come in close touch with that. To this remarkable and moving evidence we must now turn.

---

9. 2 Corinthians 5:17; Galatians 6:15.

Twelve

The Resurrection in Practice

If you decided to become a Christian in the first two decades after Jesus' death, what differences might it have made to you?

You would have made your decision to do this—infants seem not to have been received. For some time you would have belonged, provisionally, to a Christian group that met regularly in your city. Now you wanted to commit yourself to the Christian life permanently.

Our Family Becomes Whole

Your group's meetings were in a room in some house—there would be no church buildings for two centuries. There the group enacted the ceremony to receive you. They thought of it as "becoming clothed, so to speak, with the life of Christ himself."

The ceremony pointed to some of the changes that sharing the life of Christ would make. "There is no difference between Jews and Gentiles, between slaves and free, between men and women. You are all one in your union with Christ Jesus."[1]

As you took off your old clothes and put on a garment symbolizing your becoming "clothed with the life of Christ himself," you were taking up the task of enabling the human family to overcome its divisions and become its true self. In your group, you would already have noticed how all felt obliged to accept all members as of equal dignity—this in a society where things like sexism were accepted as the norm. In your group, women were free to take leadership roles; a slave counted as much as his owners and could take charge of the group's money.

These weren't special laws imposed by whim on Christians. They were seen as the necessary outcome of "becoming clothed with the life of Christ himself." The purpose of a Christian group wasn't just to make its members "holy." It was to show the world what the "new creation" was like. The God whom Jesus had shown in Palestine was, through the "body" of the risen Jesus, beginning to reconstitute us as the human family we were created to be.

Power in All

We all know that power can take many forms. It can be used to destroy, to humiliate, or just for our own advantage. The power experienced here was creative, transforming. It didn't *limit* the power of other people: it always fostered it.

How widely and deeply it did that this early evidence can show us. The New Testament name for this power gives us a clue to its nature. In the 20th century that name, "the Spirit of Jesus," may suggest the disembodied. Then we remember that, in the Bible, "the Spirit" meant God's creative power in this physical and human creation. "The Spirit of Jesus," then, was that power exercised by the risen Jesus to bring about God's rule, with the warm humanity and service he had shown in Palestine. The point of becoming a Christian was to share with

---

1. The two quotations just given stem from Christian experience of this ceremony in Paul's communities. (Galatians 3:27-28)

Jesus in using that same power. You used it the way Jesus had shown: serving, showing compassion, offering welcome to all.

Some of the practical forms this took we have already noticed. We have seen them in Jesus' life, and now we see them in these Christians. It wasn't condescension to the disadvantaged or papering over divisions. Instead, it was recognition of our human kinship, with the warmth and happiness of Jesus' meals. The philosophers' dreams of a restored humanity had started to come true.

Each Being "Kindness-ed"

As in a family or any group, the first thing you might notice was the atmosphere. Paul called it a perception that all was gift, that you were embraced by God's loving kindness ("charis"). This set the quality, the essential character, of any genuinely Christian group.

Over there, in the small room, was an old person of much wisdom. Next to you was someone with a gift for quietly encouraging others. There was a man good at helping people cope with serious problems. His wife had the gift of making people feel warmly welcome. Another could help the group judge its responsibilities in the light of the Bible.[2]

Called together to be Christ's "body," in their life and actions, each member knew that their gifts were the lifeblood of the community. Those with the more impressive kind were naturally tempted to self-importance. But, when that was avoided, something remarkable emerged.

There was nothing timid or half-hearted in their use of their powers: they were acting out of the Spirit, the power and partnership of the risen Christ. The new world launched by the resurrection had been put in their hands. They had become involved in God's kindness in action—just as had the people round Jesus' tables.

---

2. This is what was meant then by the gift of prophecy (it wasn't primarily about foretelling).

Their own individuality and responsibility became more, not less—as Jesus had made clear in his *Talent* story. Paul took that sense of God's kindness and coined a word for each person's individual ability to take an important role. By being given your particular role, you had been "kindness-ed" ("charis-ma") by God. To quench the members' charisma was to kill the group's resurrection life. Then you would have something dead on your hands. (1 Thessalonians 5:19-22)

The Outcome

The boldness of the claim created great difficulties—as Jesus and his friends had found in Capharnaum and elsewhere. *Within* the groups, Paul himself called the love required "hard labor." (1 Thessalonians 1:3) *Outside* the groups, there was mounting indignation, leading to persecution. Respectable citizens were appalled by what they had heard of the social customs of this new religion: "The lax way they treat slaves and women is undermining our whole social system!"

In the shallow Greek world of the time, where prestige and pleasure were often primary, the success of these groups was vulnerable and patchy. But even with his least successful communities, Paul could appeal to their profound experience of Jesus' transforming power.

Thessalonika was one place where he had had much success. Paul describes the kind of life which they largely achieved:

They warned the idle,
encouraged the timid,
helped the weak,
and were patient with everyone.

They saw that no one paid back wrong for wrong,
but at all times made it their aim to do good to one
another and to all people. (1 Thessalonians 5:14-15)

So, realism and tenderness, practical help and fruitfulness: this was the resurrection world to which all were called.

As we think of these things, our own experience may come to mind. I think of Jean-Marie Hiesberger telling me, in 1985, of

Renew groups in Kansas City and beyond: "For the first time, people are experiencing the affirmation of their gifts." I remember the enthusiasm—even awe—with which this senior official spoke of this, as she thought of the difference this was making to many Christian lives.[3]

Even the wayward Galatians might recognize that *it was in such relationships* that Jesus' power bore its fruit. "The fruit of the Spirit is love, joy, peace, patience, kindness, goodness, faithfulness, humility, and self-control."[4] Like a rich man with his treasures, Paul savored the reality behind each word. *His* treasure was the groups he knew where such attitudes were found.

Full Humanity

Religion, we know, can stifle. It can reduce people's humanity by forbidding essential elements of healthy life. It may be fanatical, and so shut off realism and the rational. It can insist on passive obedience, at the cost of people's responsibility. It can create a self-regarding elite that despises those outside it.

The resurrection world found in Paul's communities, even at their best, could obviously never be perfect—Christian life is the beginning, not the finished article. In some social matters there were serious limitations in Paul's Christian understanding: the outreach to others, for example, was incomplete. But it is in the light of his own principles and practices that we can detect these limitations.

With these exceptions, we find an astonishing range of affirmation of the elements of healthy life. Even the brief sketch we have had room for can indicate something of its richness.

There was the way, for example, in which a group was meant to operate. Must they slavishly follow a Pauline blueprint or statements from the Bible? Would the members' responsibility

---

3. Jean-Marie Hiesberger is Director of the Institute for Pastoral Life, Kansas City, Missouri.

4. Galatians 5:22

be usurped, and their gifts be ignored or manipulated by a leader?

In fact, no one was imposed as leader, not even Paul. Occasionally, Paul would shout at them, when a crisis situation in basic discipline arose. But with those rare exceptions, he wanted them to freely make their own decisions. Paul wasn't their "father" or leader, only their "brother". He was glad to share his authority with them.

All Paul insisted on was that they made their decisions in the Christian way. That involved *everyone* taking part, according to their "charisma".

Some members of the group could remind them clearly and accurately of relevant Christian teaching ("the teachers"). Still more important were those with the gift of relating those truths to the present problems and opportunities ("the prophets").

The fact that *both* were essential tells us much about the Christian way. There was neither to be blind application of official teaching, nor merely cutting your sails to contemporary winds.

Anyone with a gift of prophecy or teaching was entitled to perform those functions—the chief leadership roles in any group. They weren't "the people with all the answers". They must defer to others with similar gifts. The whole community must evaluate and decide. Depth, realism and loving sharing: all were essential in any group. Those weren't nice theories in pious books, but the everyday business of ordinary Christians.

To act in that way was, of course, demanding: "the *hard labor* of love" was the common experience. But only in that way can love be real: the respectful warm sharing of values, insights, difficulties and action. In the struggle and partial successes of bringing this to birth, you felt the costly support of these people's "love, joy, peace and patience". You experienced their "faithfulness," in spite of wrongs or misunderstandings. You saw their "humility and self-control". Never again could these seem to you a mere list from a book. Jesus' resurrection power, or "Spirit," had come to fruitfulness at the center of what you were involved in.

What does it feel like to live in that way? What difference does it make in how you see yourself in the present and future?

One way of expressing it was as a feeling of *being at home*. As you looked at the world, you knew that "all belongs to you," for "God will give you all that he has for his sons and daughters."[5]

The basis of this conviction was the knowledge that "God has sent the Spirit of his Son into your hearts"[6]—an experience Paul could appeal to even in the Galatians. In themselves and in others, they knew the Spirit of the risen Jesus: "the reality of the raised Christ in so far as the raised Christ is experienced."[7] You found this at the heart of your striving to make the world more human.

Jesus had spent his public life announcing that the Rule of God was breaking into the world, and showing, through his life, what it is like. The symbol for the same reality was now "the Spirit". Jesus had experienced God's Rule as most personal: the intimate and creative closeness of his Father. His followers had experienced it through Jesus' own self. And now this same power, in Christians' hands, was the presence of the risen Jesus. "If Christ lives in you, then the Spirit is life for you"; and "if the Spirit of God, who raised Jesus from death, lives in you, then he who raised Christ from death will also give life to your mortal bodies by the presence of his Spirit in you."[8]

This power tended to be described as "Spirit," rather than as "Jesus," to indicate that he now lived in the fullness of the risen life: a fullness he was now enabling men and women to fashion in themselves, as they struggled to bring for all the human family the "new creation" to birth.

The Meaning

The significance of this can be lost sight of in two ways.

---

5. 1 Corinthians 3:21 and Galatians 4:7
6. Galatians 4:6
7. Peter Carnley, *The Structure of Resurrection Belief*, Oxford, 1988, p. 256.
8. Romans 8:10, 11

Largely because it can't be expressed without the help of symbols, it can seem to be unreal: a "religious" world distracting from the real world, an escape from the tasks that face humanity.

This occupational hazard of religions has, very obviously, not been avoided by Christianity. But what Jesus and Paul show so clearly is that the opposite was intended.

Jesus was a layman with no home whose concern was to heal and welcome all. Paul was a Christian "brother" whose only wish was to help all grow through the presence of the risen Christ. People who did that "shared their belongings with their needy fellow-Christians and opened their homes to strangers. They were happy with those who are happy, and wept with those who weep. They had the same concern for everyone."[9]

This compassionate, practical outreach was not imposed from "headquarters". Each individual's and group's task was to discern the will of God in the light of their gifts and the local situation. True, the human goodness being sought would be only partly achieved. Our own limitations and that of the situation make completeness unattainable. But the experience of God's Spirit in the name of Jesus had shown that this was only "the first installment."[10] "He will change our weak mortal bodies and make them like his own, using that power by which he is able to bring all things under his rule."[11]

To miss the *sheer humanity* of the whole enterprise is one way of losing sight of its significance. The other way is to forget what the witnesses meant when they called this "resurrection."

We can see this as an "unearthly," rather arbitrary handout for Christians: a dispensable, perhaps elitist, appendix to our story. Contributing to such a view is a picture of God. He is like the chairperson of an international company communicating, through fax and telex, with a minor branch in a remote country.

Yet Jesus' assertion was that the chairperson was "Father," intimately creative in our midst. The Christian assertion is that

9. Romans 12:13-15

10. 2 Corinthians 1:22

11. Philippians 3:21

God in his power lives and is known at the center of our striving.

Calling this experience "resurrection" says that this is no arbitrary appendix. It claims that to be true to himself and to his creatures God *had* to lead all to this climax. It was the full expression of God's true self, of his very integrity. It was also the full expression of our true and good humanity.

When the significance of this is grasped, only one attitude is possible. In his prison cell in Ephesus, hourly awaiting the death sentence, Paul wrote to the Philippians to share with them his joy. "I share my joy with you all; you too must share your joy with me. May you always be joyful in your union with the Lord. And God's peace, which is far beyond human understanding, will stand guard over your minds and hearts in union with Christ Jesus. The God who gives peace will be with you."[12]

---

12. Philippians 2:17,18; 4:4,7,9.

Thirteen

What *Do* the Gospels Say?

Was all this founded on fact or on fiction? And if it was on fact, what could it mean for us?

Up to now we have focused on the earliest evidence about the resurrection. We noted the change in Jesus' friends from despair to great confidence. They described the experience that caused that change as "God has raised Jesus from the dead." This meant not just survival but "the first installment" of the full coming of God's personality and power.[1] To see whether this was more than pious theory, we looked at the lives of some ordinary Christians in the early 50s. To the extent that they allowed this power into their lives, what difference did it make?

We saw that it didn't quench their humanity, but made them more richly human. It didn't suppress such characteristics as integrity, love and faithfulness, but affirmed them, encouraged them, and brought them to full flower. Sometimes that was in world-wide projects, like the rediscovery of our human kinship. Sometimes it was in using your gifts and responsibility in simply

---

1. 2 Corinthians 1:22; 5:5

everyday actions. Jesus' resurrection was the event that launched this transformation.

But what was the experience that gave rise to this? And what about the Gospel stories? By answering these questions, we shall be closer to understanding the real nature of the Jesus story, both in the New Testament itself and in its relevance to us today.

What Kind of Experience

What kind of experience led the earliest Christians to proclaim that "Jesus is risen"? To find an answer, we naturally turn to the Gospel accounts of Jesus' appearing after his resurrection. Haven't we here a description of the "appearances" that Paul mentions as the basis of the resurrection claims? We know that they are much later than the evidence we have been surveying—John's Gospel comes from 70 years later than the crucifixion. But wouldn't the accounts of such key experiences have been carefully preserved?

Some may not turn to these accounts with all the confidence they would like to have. Are we intended to take them as "photographically accurate"? If so, what should we make of the fact that the various accounts cannot be squared with one another?[2] And if a photographic record is all that they offer, what could these accounts prove? Would they prove more than "God just moved a corpse out of a tomb and made Jesus alive again"?[3] We have already seen abundant evidence that the claim being made by the resurrection of Jesus was very much more. It was that "God had found his way to being all in all and overcoming everything that stands in the way of this."[4]

Those words are the Bishop of Durham's, but he is simply paraphrasing Paul. Paul never mentions the tomb nor gives any

---

2. "The number and names of the women, the number of their visits to the grave, the number of the angels, all change . . . . No harmonization is possible." (Walter Kasper, *Jesus the Christ*, London & New York, 1976, p. 149)

3. David E. Jenkins, Bishop of Durham, *God, Jesus and Life in the Spirit*, London, 1988, pp. 112.

4. David Jenkins, op. cit., p. 108.

photographic descriptions of the appearances. But he was totally fired by the conviction that Jesus' resurrection power, the Spirit, was filling the world, so that "God will rule completely over all." (1 Corinthians 15:28) That conviction was his whole inspiration and support, even in the gravest dangers. Even when he wrote to the Romans whom he had never met, he could take it for granted that the same conviction was in them. His letters show it was the thrust and mainstay of the communities he founded.

This was the case, as we have just recalled, for the homely details of their lives, as well as for their involvement in wider issues, and for their view of the future. Jesus' resurrection wasn't just the restoration of a friend: "it blazed forth into the whole world and into eternity."[5] Could such a claim arise from an ordinary meeting with a friend who had merely survived death?

When we turn to the Gospels themselves, we find that they fully share that doubt. Once we get close to them, we realize that a photographic-type description was simply not their aim. They realized that an encounter with Jesus, in his risen and transforming power, was far beyond our present powers of description. The focus of their interest was in the *significance* of that encounter, not in *any details* of what was seen or heard.

The Gospels

We could start with the oldest Gospel, Mark's, written between 65 and 70. After his account of Jesus' death and burial, Mark ends his Gospel with a visit of three women to Jesus' tomb.[6]

As we look at this short account—the climax of Mark's Gospel, we are immediately struck by a surprising discovery: *there is no description of an appearance of the risen Jesus!* Mark offered his Gospel as an account of "the Good News about Jesus Christ" (1:1); and he is entirely clear that this consists of the fact that Jesus was raised from the dead. He knew that this had

---

5. David Jenkins, op. cit., p. 106.

6. Scholars are in general agreement that Mark's Gospel originally ended at 16:8. 16:9-20 was added some decades later.

been shown by the "appearances" of the risen Jesus (16:7), but felt no necessity to describe any such appearance.

We don't have to *guess* why Mark offers no such description. He indicates that the resurrection had a meaning that could not be expressed in the kind of meeting we can describe. He does this by putting the announcement of the resurrection in the mouth of a "heavenly" figure—the Bible's stock way of suggesting an event with a God-like dimension:[7] the dimension that gives true meaning to all time and all people.

Mark has led up to that announcement by taking a story of a visit of some women to Jesus' tomb and adding other elements that help him to present the proclamation of the resurrection.

Matthew's account shows an equal freedom in transmuting Mark's material so as to bring out its significance to *his* readers. Mark's young man becomes more clearly an angel: God himself in visible form. An earthquake is introduced into Mark's account so as to underline the cosmic, universal importance.

Matthew's purpose is to stress the God-like dimension of the resurrection, not to paint the scene as a television crew would have filmed it. In fact, his use of an angel would have made this even clearer to his readers, since in an Old Testament scene he was echoing, only the person attuned to that dimension "saw" the vision: "the men who were with me did not see anything." (Daniel 10:7) A television crew would have had to report: "No pictures"!

The job the four Gospel writers had in hand was to take the "jewel" of the Good News, which their communities shared with them, and display it in such a way as to show forth its sheer wonder and meaning. Part of the material they used for this was stories they had received about women visiting Jesus' tomb. Like virtually all historians until four centuries ago, they were much more interested in significance than in recording precisely what happened.[8] That there *had* been "appearances" of the risen

---

7. The white robe of the young man would have indicated to Mark's readers a "heavenly" being. So would the women's reaction of "amazement," and other features of the account.

8. Fifteen centuries later, in England, that would still be the case in the historians Shakespeare used as the basis of his History Plays. If they approved

Jesus they were entirely sure. The point now was to explore and present their meaning as fully as they could.

Using Old Stories

The Gospel writers had two main points they wanted to make about the meaning. Since they were story writers, not textbook writers, they made these points in story form. The Old Testament happened to provide them with just what they needed. For over 700 years, it had expressed encounters between God and people by means of graphic stories.

The Gospel writers knew that their readers would recognize the familiar pattern and enter into its drift. It seemed the best framework available in which to set off the Good News.

There was the story, for example, in Genesis when Abraham looked out of his tent and saw God[9]—though he didn't immediately recognize him. Abraham's response was to offer him the amenities of Oriental hospitality: water to wash feet, a rest, and the best meal that could be had. We get the bustle in the kitchen at the sudden arrival of an important guest: "Quick, Sarah; take a sack of your best flour, and bake some bread." (Genesis 18:6)

What is being expressed by such graphic touches is the Hebrew's sense of *God's closeness*. But this and the similar stories had another major interest. God wasn't just close to us, offering fellowship and comfort. *God had a plan for his world, and his people had the main role in that.*

That is brought out in the other dimension to these stories: there is more than just the *visual*, there are also the *verbal* messages. So Moses is told, in a similar story, "to lead my people out of Egypt and take them to a rich and fertile land." (Exodus 3:10,17) Gideon, in another story, is told to "go with all your great strength and rescue my people" from the country's oppressors, who were devastating the land and making the Israelites hide in caves. (Judges 6:14) In one way or another, these appearance stories were about *God giving a task, a commission*, as

---

of a king politically, they felt free to invent for him admirable qualities!

9. At first, in the guise of three men.

well as being both a close friend and a God of awesome greatness.

Obviously, this familiar kind of story was a gift to the Gospel writers. The resurrection, they believed, had established the same kind of presence. It was something that could not be told in everyday language, but could be conveyed by echoing these familiar stories.

It was God, both intimate and awesome, who had "appeared" through the risen Jesus. God's creative power, or "Spirit," was being experienced as never before. But, as in those Old Testament stories, this hadn't been just for the enrichment of the few. It was to help people stand with God and face the world's needs.

This presentation of the resurrection *as a task given to us* is in fact the main thrust of these Gospel stories. "As the Father sent me, so I am sending you." (John 20:21) "Go, therefore, and make disciples of all nations." (Matthew 28:19) These commissions were directed to *all* Christians, not just to a group of leaders.

The Gospel writers didn't invent this main thrust: it had been Paul's experience decades before. When Paul had "seen" the risen Jesus, it was "so that I might preach the Good News about him to the Gentiles." (Galatians 1:16) Again, the Gospels weren't trying to give Christians *information* they didn't already have, but to help them understand these truths more deeply and practically in their own time and place.

Each writer is conscious of trying to express the inexpressible. He wants to capture a little more of the inexhaustible meaning. Every touch, every detail, is arranged to that end. Like the finest music, we can "hear" them as often as we wish and catch fresh nuances and insights about what the resurrection means.

We turned to the Gospels to ask the question: What experience gave rise to the Christian conviction about the resurrection? What we have found is that the Gospel accounts were not written to answer that question. The reason why each account is so different isn't carelessness. Each writer was simply doing what his readers would expect of him: shaping an appearance-of-God story to illuminate for them the most splendid "appearance" of all.

Though not trying to answer our question, do the Gospels throw some *indirect* light on it?

They do use material that is often much older than themselves. But it hasn't yet been possible to be sure when they are giving us access to the earliest accounts.

Don't they at least show that the original experiences must have been physical? True, the Old Testament stories felt free to describe "appearances" of God as quite physical; but don't Luke's and John's stories emphasize the physical much more than those?

Yes, they *do* put greater stress on the physical than did the Old Testament stories; but we have to remember why. Recognition of the person appearing was a major strand in this kind of story. In the "appearance" of Jesus, the person was a human being: one whom his followers had heard, seen and touched. The stress on the physical was necessary in order to emphasize the continuity between their friend and the risen person they had "seen." "I am he" is one of the central points in Luke's resurrection story. (24:39)

Back to the Early Evidence

If we demand from a daughter or son a talent they don't possess, we may fail to recognize their real ability. If we demand from the Gospels to tell us of the original experience, it may be difficult for us to take from them what they actually seek to offer us. We may also fail to notice evidence that relates much more closely to our question.

Decades before the Gospels were written, Christians were trying to express the meaning of the experience that had been had of the risen Jesus. One way of expressing it, as we have seen, was as "resurrection," and another as the coming to us of "God's Spirit."[10]

"Resurrection" matched their experience of God expressing his love, faithfulness and creative power in all that had happened in Jesus and in their present lives; "Spirit" expressed much the

---

10. Namely, "God as He makes himself known" (Peter Carnley, op. cit., p. 310).

same realization, with more focus on the present transforming effect of this power. *Both* expressed their sense that human history had now reached its climax. Both Resurrection and the coming of the Spirit had long been seen as the time when all would come to fulfillment: when God, the life-giver, would come in his inexpressible richness.

Their overwhelming sense of God's closeness reinforced this conviction. The battle *had* been won—though the fruits of victory could not yet be fully gathered. That must wait until our bodily existence had been transformed in the same way as Jesus'.

The center of interest, we notice, was more on God's activity than on Jesus'. The earliest creed was "God has raised Jesus from the dead." The stress was on God's life-giving power, which had now been fully exerted in that human life.

We can watch the first Christians beginning to work out the implications of that in the very first decade. It forced them to ask the question: *Who exactly was the person in whom that event has happened?*

One solution seems to have come to them through their combining two things they knew. One was the fact that Jesus had been condemned to death as the Messiah ("the King of the Jews"). True, Jesus had not claimed that title. In Jesus' time, it would have been seen as demanding armed revolt against the Romans. But the title had been his accusers' charge against Jesus of having such intentions.

After his death, his friends realized how appropriate the title was. Even in those times it spoke of power that went far beyond the merely political. "He shall gather a holy people"; "he will shepherd the flock of the Lord faithfully": these would be the tasks of the Messiah as much as "purging Jerusalem from the foreigners."[11]

The role of the Messiah was to come and exercise God's own power. God would say to his Messiah:

---

11. From the Psalms of Solomon, 17: written about 70 years before, but very influential in Jesus' time.

> You are my son;
> Today I have become your father.
> Ask, and I will give you all the nations;
> the whole earth will be yours.
> (Psalm 2:7-8)

The old Jewish songs caught many glimpses of *the kind of kingdom* this might be:

> Your kingdom is founded on integrity and justice,
> love and faithfulness are shown in all you do.
> (Psalm 89:15)

Now the Christians found this reality growing in their midst through the power of the risen Jesus. Wasn't he clearly the Messiah, the promised king, sent in God's power to "all the nations"?

So, once again we see that Jesus' resurrection, for the earliest Christians, had essentially to do with *God's kind of power*. They had become convinced of the presence of this power through the combination of two things. One was Jesus' "appearances"; the other was their own ongoing Christian experience.

But how describe an encounter with a person which convinced you that this inexpressible power was here? Could merely seeing a human shape and hearing human language have conveyed such certainty of the presence of this power?

Something objective was there—the word Paul uses for "appear" conveys that. Something was "seen" that was external to the person having the experience.[12] Paul also insists that the new life of Jesus—and eventually of us—has a fuller kind of *bodiliness*: one "filled by the Spirit." (1 Corinthians 15:44) But when asked "What kind of body," he doesn't supply a physical description, as one might expect, of the kind of body he saw in Jesus on the Damascus road. There is no sure evidence of such a description in the Gospels, as we have seen.

The point of our bodiliness, we remember, is our ability to relate to people and things: it's not primarily our having a particular size and shape. The bodiliness of the risen Jesus who

---

12. See 1 Corinthians 9:1; 1 Corinthians 15:8. The word has recently been discussed by Peter Carnley, op. cit., 227-231, 242-243.

related to all: can we be sure it would have looked like ours? If not, the difficulties of describing it could obviously be insurmountable.

From the physical point of view, this is all that the witnesses clearly say about the original experiences. Whatever physical dimensions those experiences may have had were not their main interest, and seem to have been indescribable. Their interest was in the amazing discovery that their friend and master was not a failure but "the life-giving Spirit"; that our destiny is to be "modeled" on him;[13] and that the story of the whole human race had now reached its final stage.

Appreciating this opens out for us a much fuller kind of Christian life. In the past, "Resurrection" tended to mean little more than a picture of Jesus' physical appearances nearly 2,000 years ago. A mainly past event cannot be the central inspiration of our lives, so that "prayer and worship (could become) dutiful consequences of belief, not responses to his perceived presence."[14]

But what the Scriptures do is to show Jesus' resurrection as life-giving, both then and always. "If Christ lives in you, the Spirit is life for you." (Romans 8:10) It is the dynamic center of history: God expressing himself fully in the whole world. The Jesus story was going on, even more strongly, and all were invited to accept a part in it. This was the discovery we find the Scriptures struggling to express.

---

13. 1 Corinthians 15:45, 49

14. Peter Carnley, op. cit., p. 27 (parenthesis mine)

Fourteen

The Empty Tomb— and the Media

All this naturally raises a question that has recently been passionately discussed. I have suggested that the early evidence for the resurrection gives no clear message whether the risen Jesus was seen physically. Doesn't that suggestion ignore the evidence of the empty tomb?

"Media Vision"

Over this question most of the media has cast its baleful spell. Only by noticing that spell and avoiding it can we get at the answers.

The media deals with biblical matters differently from other topics. The better interviewer or journalist will normally take considerable trouble to get briefed before a broadcast or an article. Very few will do the same for any topic connected with the Scriptures. They simply assume that the Bible is to be taken as literally as a handbook on car maintenance. Any other kind of attempt to come to grips with the deeper meaning of our lives is allowed to have several layers of meaning: music, art, literature, things of that kind. But the Bible must be as straightforward as a recipe on a supermarket box.

So "the good guys" are those who interpret the Bible in that way, and "the bad guys" are those who claim that the Bible writers used things like symbols and other literary devices. Such things are all right in TV advertisements, plays, and any form of expression of any depth. But someone who attributes them to the Bible is watering down Christianity, is a devious trickster, and, if a Church leader, should be made to resign.

Such an approach not only ignores all the patient work done by thousands of scholars on the Bible over the last 60 years. It also makes it impossible for the Bible, and the event of the resurrection, to utter their message about the presence among us of the transcendent God. It is like insisting that all music critics must be tone-deaf or all sports commentators blind.

Of course, like most standpoints, it is expressing some valid insights. It is correctly stressing that Christianity, and the resurrection, are about our bodiliness and our world, and that symbols *have* often been used to dilute the human realism of the Christian message. What it fatally neglects is that symbols, as every lover or artist knows, are the only means we have of opening our minds and hearts to the human meaning of our existence. Symbols, biblical scholarship, almost anything can be abused. But do we ban cars—or even love—just because they can be dangerous?

What the media usually does is to take this natural but sterile tendency and encourage it to be the norm. We have to free ourselves from "media vision" to see the empty tomb in true perspective.

The Empty Tomb

As soon as we do, certain obvious landmarks are seen and we begin to get our bearings. Let's assume that we know something about the climate of Palestine and about the decomposition of corpses. This shows us that Mark's making the women come to the tomb to anoint the body two days after the burial cannot be intended as literally true. Mark has more important business on his hands than the literal reporting of the physical action of anointing a corpse. He wants to show vividly, in story form, the women's attachment to Jesus, and their complete lack of expectation of what in fact happened. We have already seen how other non-literal elements, like the angel, were well-known devices to suggest the God-like dimension of the event.

There *is* an empty tomb in Mark's story, and the women notice it is empty. But Mark doesn't make them conclude from *that* to the resurrection. Only contact with something more than the merely physical can open up that insight, whether the "angel's" announcement, or an "appearance."

Of course, it doesn't follow from this that the tomb wasn't found empty. We will come to that question when we have assembled enough evidence. At present, the media and other influences are preventing us from looking objectively at that evidence. The fact that Mark does not give it central importance, and Paul does not mention it at all, should at least make the discussion become a bit more relaxed!

Other factors we've already noticed can increase our feeling that this question is not in fact a "make-or-break" issue. It is clear that the event called by the early witnesses "resurrection" was something much greater, much more real, than could be *proven* by the resuscitation of a dead body. And none of the early witnesses, in fact, uses it as a proof.

But though it cannot be a proof, is it a necessary condition? Is a claim that Jesus is risen *compatible* with his body's decomposing in a tomb?

When we had a picture of Jesus' resurrection as an event that easily fitted into the categories by which we understand and control things, we naturally thought we understood it well enough to tell what it *must* involve. The witnesses saw Jesus physically; so his physical body could not have remained in the tomb.[1]

Now the earliest evidence has shown us that what was experienced was a presence of Jesus that goes far beyond our nor-

---

1. Also it was thought that first-century Jews could not have accepted the event as "resurrection" if Jesus' body had still been there. This is now known to be untrue—though still repeated in the media!

mal categories. It was a *bodily* presence: one of a whole human person. But it would be arrogant to claim that our physical kind of bodily presence is the only one there is, or that it can certainly make available to us the more real and creative presence found in Jesus—and promised to us at *our* resurrection (when our bodies will have become ashes or decomposed).

What all this shows is that a person who equates the reality of the resurrection with the empty tomb has probably failed to understand what the witnesses claimed to have happened. It is to reduce the human reality of the resurrection to a shred of its true self.

Once we have taken this on board, we can cope adequately with the question. Research has shown that the story of the empty tomb was much older than the Gospels. Originally it wasn't connected with the appearance stories—and certainly wasn't used as a proof of the resurrection. Probably, but not certainly, there was a visit to the tomb. But the data simply can't *prove* that the original event consisted of finding the tomb empty. Nor can it *prove* that this old story originated from an actual visit. Several scholars believe that it arose from an annual ceremony at the tomb to celebrate the fact of Jesus' resurrection.[2]

Three conclusions therefore seem to arise from our inquiry into the story of the empty tomb. One is that it would be dishonest to claim that the tomb was certainly empty. Another is that it would be foolish to deny that there is *some* (but not conclusive) evidence that it was empty. But the greatest folly would be *to make a necessary connection* between the empty tomb and the resurrection. Only those who choose to ignore the Scriptures

---

2. For example: "The contemporary situation giving rise to the account was a liturgical celebration of the Jerusalem community. . . . It seems, therefore, that at first the Christians did not know, or at least did not speak, of an empty tomb. This was most probably so because on the basis of their Easter experience they realized that the resurrection was altogether different from the resuscitation of a corpse from a tomb. Neither for the Christians who believed in the resurrection nor for the Jews who understood but rejected their message had an empty tomb any relevance." (Herman Hendrickx, *Resurrection Narratives*, London, 1984, p. 18-19).

can make such a connection. And we don't usually give much credence to people who build houses from straw.

Media Vision: an Example

We can get at the facts about Jesus only by listening to what the Bible is really saying. But TV and radio are part of the air we breathe, and while they refuse to do that listening, it can make it more difficult for us to do that ourselves.

The best way to avoid this problem may be to take a specific example. Once we have noticed how the media can trivialize the Bible, we are less likely to be affected. In fact, their ways of reducing it to car-maintenance-book level become quite amusing.

We could take as our example a program, in 1986, when one of two interviewers involved began by asking a Christian leader[3] about the resurrection: "What actually happened?" "I know what actually happened," this leader replied. "Various people had various encounters with Jesus which totally convinced them that he was really alive in a transformed way." So, Jesus was alive: the carpenter from Nazareth. He was alive with the creative power of God to transform all humanity. Couldn't the interviewers understand that he was simply paraphrasing the evidence to be found in the Scriptures? Or couldn't they have read what he had written the year before: "I do believe in the Resurrection of Jesus Christ our Lord from the dead. I myself live in the hope of that Resurrection"?

But the interviewers had no intention of missing the opportunity of controversy or even scandal. They insisted that if you didn't take all the Gospels literally, you didn't believe anything they said.

If they had taken the trouble to brief themselves at all, they would have known that no serious Scripture scholar accepts that. If they had even bothered to read the Gospels, they would have seen that the Gospels themselves often choose not to interpret each other literally! They felt quite free to retell stories, to add or subtract details, to give a different slant. This wasn't at

---

3. David Jenkins, the Bishop of Durham.

all because they disagreed with the Christian beliefs that the other Gospels presented. But they realized that no single statement could express for any of them its full reality and significance. You had to turn it this way and that, and view it from many angles. Symbols and poetry would help open out the deeper perspectives.

But the Gospels themselves had no apparent interest to these interviewers. Instead, they stuck to "literal, or heresy" with bloodthirsty tenacity. Heresy in a Christian leader? How the media would howl!

All the bishop was actually doing was to insist on the deeper understanding of resurrection that biblical scholarship is opening up. "It is perfectly reasonable to believe in God's raising of Jesus, and for me it is overwhelming." "The very life and purpose and personality which was in him was actually continuing." "The resurrection of Jesus Christ is about God finding his way to being all in all and overcoming everything that stands in the way of this." Is this the language of someone "abolishing the whole foundation of the Christian faith"?

"All right," some responsible person might reply. "Going beyond the purely literal isn't to destroy the foundations themselves. But would not the simple, trusting faith of many millions of Christians be brutally destroyed?"

Whatever our answer to that question, we notice what it implies. It implies that many of the Churches have done little to help the members interpret Bible teaching, even on the resurrection, the most central of all Christian truths. What chance, we may ask, have those outside the Church been given of understanding the Christian "Good News," intended for all the world?

Of course, there is truth in the objection. Our deepest understanding of profound things can't change overnight. But if resurrection lies at the heart of the Christian message to all the world, dare we evade frank and public discussion?

Conclusion

In a meal in an ill-lit room, in a welcoming smile or a courageous stand, in such things as these, Jesus claimed, people could see the fullness of God. And all this was part, he maintained, of a wider thing: God's People becoming whole, and renewed for the world.

His contemporaries were looking for a "knock-down" God. From far above the battle, God would force the Romans out. It was unthinkable that God could be *most* present through a man like Jesus, siding with sinners in their deepest longings and needs. It was unthinkable that God's fullest presence could be subject to human approval, and meet the rejection of the cross.

If we think of the Jesus story as being just about a holy individual, we picture God as being "above" it, only *in*directly involved. But biblical scholarship is gradually disclosing to us a different view.

The resurrection of Jesus is more than the end of an individual's story. It is "a declaration of God, through a particular man, of his eternal nature, his persistent purpose and his all-embracing promise. . . . This God entrusts himself to men and women in their freedom and in the consequent sin and risks collaboration with them."[4]

Has sharing ever been closer? Has fellowship ever been more intimate and strong?

---

4. David E. Jenkins, op. cit., p. 106-107